Praise for *You Are Not Stuck*

"Each of us has the capacity _____ ie world, but we need the ini_____ e meaningful and lasting cha_____ ch for revealing your own courage and grace, this book is perfectly poised to help you make choices—and believe in yourself— with confidence and clarity."

—Elena Brower, bestselling author of *Practice You*

"Feeling stuck and scared is a totally gross but totally normal part of real motherf*cking life, and there's no shame in needing help. We all do from time to time. In *You Are Not Stuck*, Becky Vollmer holds out a hand—an insightful, grace-filled, relentlessly human hand—to pull you out of the suckery and turn your fear into fuel for bold choices. I love the energy of this book."

—Jennifer Pastiloff, author of *On Being Human*

"With openness, compassion and earned optimism, Becky Vollmer guides us out of paralysis into action, reminding us that *stuck* is a state of mind, and that choice is where our real power lives. For anyone needing to make a change in their lives but not sure how to begin, get this energizing and important book immediately and let Becky hold your hand as you discover just how ready and powerful you are."

—Scott Stabile, author of *Big Love*

"An earnest exhortation to pursue one's passions."

—*Publisher's Weekly*

"It's difficult to imagine anyone for whom this wisdom wouldn't be helpful." —Spirituality & Practice

"Becky Vollmer has written a brave and deeply wise wake-up call-to-empowerment that will change the lives of every person who picks it up. In a warm, often uproarious voice reminiscent of Anne Lamott, *You Are Not Stuck* is the book we need right now to guide us through the psychic quicksand that keeps us from moving forward in our lives and fulfilling our potential. I loved it, I learned from it, and I'm passing it on to everyone I know." —Elissa Altman, author of *Motherland*

"*You Are Not Stuck* is both the balm and boost I didn't know I needed. While self-development authors often struggle with the 'how' of change, Becky has managed to turn it art: a practical, humble, and humorous invitation to reclaim your life— instructions absolutely included!"
—Dr. Rebecca Ray, clinical psychologist and author

"This isn't just another self-help read, filled with the same listicle of pseudo-empowerment tips to manifest your own destiny. *You Are Not Stuck* is a conversation with friend; a friend who encourages you to evaluate your own priorities, and understand that there is nothing wrong with where you are on your path. Honest, empowering, and freeing. A must-read!"
—Emily Lynn Paulson, author of *Highlight Real*

you are not STUCK

How Soul-Guided Choices Transform Fear into Freedom

BECKY VOLLMER

ST. MARTIN'S
ESSENTIALS
NEW YORK

For The Sisters,
the ones
who changed
everything.

Published in the United States by St. Martin's Essentials,
an imprint of St. Martin's Publishing Group

www.stmartins.com

Designed by Steven Seighman

The Library of Congress Cataloging-in-Publication Data
is available upon request.

ISBN 978-1-250-86438-3 (trade paperback)

Our books may be purchased in bulk for promotional, educational, or business
use. Please contact your local bookseller or the Macmillan Corporate and
Premium Sales Department at 1-800-221-7945, extension 5442,
or by email at MacmillanSpecialMarkets@macmillan.com.

First St. Martin's Essentials Trade Paperback Edition: 2024

10 9 8 7 6 5 4 3 2 1

Contents

Introduction

The best thing you can possibly do with your life is to tackle the motherfucking shit out of it.
—Cheryl Strayed

On an exceptionally bright and warm January morning in 2013, a friend and I walked the beach at San Francisco's Crissy Field toward the Golden Gate Bridge. It was abuzz with walkers and runners, dogs with their Frisbees and their people. I suspected most visitors would pause to soak up the sunshine and bountiful view, but all I could do was wonder, with more than a hint of scorn: *It's Friday. Why aren't all these people at work?*

For me, it was the start of a long-anticipated girls' weekend—with Napa Valley wine tastings and a Calistoga mud bath in our future—yet there I was, my St. Louis feet in California sand, spending what should have been quality vacation time pissing and moaning, once again, about my job. My specific lament: the never-ending, emotionally draining push-pull between work and family.

"Maybe I could reduce my schedule even more?" I speculated to my friend Chelsey as we strolled. "Or work exclusively for one client . . . or move to human resources . . . or *something*?"

But every idea was a square peg in a round hole, and I knew it. Sometimes bad can't be made better.

At that moment, I spied a family playing at the water's edge. A man threw a ball with his young son, who I guessed was almost the same age as my younger daughter, then just three. The man scooped up the giggling boy, tossed him high against the sun, and hugged him in close. I immediately felt a pang from having missed too many of those moments with my girls.

That's what I want. Not this. THAT. I stopped walking and sobbed.

"Listen," Chelsey said firmly. "If you're that unhappy doing what you're doing, then do something different. And if that doesn't work out, do something different again. You're smart, you're marketable. You'll figure it out."

I swear my jaw hit the ground so hard that sand stuck in my teeth. I was a nearly forty-year-old mother of two who counseled C-suite executives at Fortune 500 companies—and I truly hadn't realized that choosing another path was an option.

Was she suggesting I could walk away from something I didn't like, even though I'd spent more than a decade cultivating it? Did she just give me permission . . . to quit?

Permission to quit, to change, to live in alignment with priorities that had evolved as *I* had evolved, to redefine what success looked like for me—that was the permission she gave me, all right. And from the moment just four days later when I sat down in my boss's office and resigned, it has been my mission to give that permission to everyone else.

Because we all *have* choices; we just have to be brave enough to *make* them.

The Backstory

For almost a dozen years, I'd toiled at one of the world's top public relations agencies, grinding my way from an entry-level account executive to a partner-track senior vice president leading a multimillion-dollar global practice. I was good, and I was going places. Yet I was *fried*. I could barely string two sentences together. My polished persona was nothing but a veneer.

Other people liked me and my work. But I didn't like the person I had become.

I tried to blame work-life balance, or the lack of it. Before children, I was a workhorse, an Energizer bunny, a machine. I. Did. Not. Stop. When I ate lunch, I usually did so at my desk while continuing to work, what my friend Hannah likes to call dining *al desko*. In my earliest years at the agency, I was among the first in the office, often arriving before the sun, and among the last to go home after the sky had turned dark again. I always felt a lonely pang when someone from the late-night cleaning crew knocked on my door and took the day's trash.

Once, when I was still pretty junior, I told my supervisor I needed to work from home the next day to wait for the cable guy. There wasn't anything that resembled "working from home" back then, at least not at that agency.

"You'll have to take a vacation day," he said.

"But I'm not going on vacation," I said. "I have tons of work to do. I just need to do it from home while I wait for the guy to show up."

"You'll have to take a vacation day," he repeated.

What utter bullshit, I thought. *Without fail, I work far more than the mandatory minimum of fifty hours a week and don't complain when the clock starts over at zero on Monday morning. I'm available to you 24/7. Where's the give and take?*

Things got trickier after I became a parent. I had been at the agency for about six years when my husband Dave and I decided to go for it. Funny thing was, I'd never planned on being a mom. In fact, for as long as I could remember, I was adamant that I did not want to have children: *They're loud, they're expensive, and there's nothing I want to teach anyone,* I thought. Throughout my twenties, my mother encouraged me to at least keep the door open to the idea.

"You never know when you might change your mind," she said. And she was right. I arrived at my early thirties, looked around at my friends with kids who didn't seem *completely* miserable, and decided to try.

The runup to motherhood had been difficult. My first pregnancy, at age thirty-three, was a complicated one due to what's called an "incompetent" cervix. (I really can't think of a worse way to get a cervix to cooperate than by calling it incompetent, can you?) That meant two key things. First, I had to get a pessary, which is kind of like an inflatable rubber donut that gets inserted through the vagina and past the cervix to sit at the base of the uterus so that baby won't, essentially, fall out. And each Tuesday for roughly six months, Dave would haul me to the doctor's office to have that lovely little pessary taken out, sterilized, and put back in. I'll spare you the details, but let me just say that having someone screw around with your very sensitive cervix on a weekly basis isn't exactly how one hopes to spend a pregnancy. I maintain that self-medicating with Harvest Grain 'N Nut pancakes from IHOP after every visit was an entirely appropriate response.

The second thing this meant was that, at all times outside of Pessary Tuesday, I was confined to bedrest. The doctor limited trips up and down the steps to once a day—a restriction that would have been more manageable had our lone bathroom not been situated on the second floor—so I spent most of my time in my bedroom. On the rare days that I'd move the party to the first floor, I peed in a medical commode my husband lovingly placed in the dining room. This went on for three months (also not the way one hopes to spend a pregnancy). I did work from home for a while, but only because the doctor insisted, and then shifted to long-term disability status until the baby came.

Waiting for my daughter to arrive wasn't the only thing that marked this period with uncertainty and concern: my dad, Leo, whom I loved so dearly, was dying of colon cancer. It was a slow and painful and tragic time. He spent nearly two long years in hospice care; he'd rally, then decline, so they kept extending his services. As my belly grew, he grew sicker and sicker. So, weekly, I broke the bedrest rules to sit on his couch while he took a co-deine doze in his red recliner.

As we neared my due date, I was convinced I'd be giving birth in one hospital while he died in another. But, somehow, he hung on and managed to pull his finest yellow cashmere sweater over his skeleton body for the 2 a.m. visit to the hospital while

I was in labor with Josie. *There's an elderly man in a wheelchair in the waiting room,* the nurse said. *Is it your grandfather?* Eight weeks later, my brother and I carried our dad to his bed for his final breaths. I put on his favorite recording of "Ave Maria"—a gripping Dixieland version by the Jim Cullum Jazz Band, the one I'd play again a few days later at his wake—and held his hand as I whispered a release. *It's okay. You can let go. You've done good.*

I'm going to take a beat here and place my hand over my heart, close my eyes, and breathe deep. And if your story includes a chapter like this, I suspect you may need a pause, too. Take it. Breathe with me. Honor your loved one, honor your sadness. It's got to have a place to go, and I highly recommend *out* over *down*. *Out* allows it to pass through you, to keep your emotional and energetic channels open and alive. *Down* makes you feel heavy and stagnant and . . . stuck.

Two weeks before my dad died—and just seven weeks into this massively confusing life with a newborn, full of sleeplessness and wonder and all the postpartum emotions—I got a call from my boss at the PR agency.

"We need you to come back," he said.

"What's going on?" I asked, surprised. I had arranged to take the full twelve weeks of unpaid maternity leave afforded by federal law, and this was just past the midway point. "Client in crisis?"

"Nothing out of the ordinary," he said. "It's just time."

All these years later, I am as floored now as I was in that

moment by the audacity of those three words—*it's just time*—
and in my heart, there was a shift. I saw my work relationship
for exactly what it was: I was a commodity, a revenue generator.
I may have sucked it up and returned to the office—just a week
after my father died—but I certainly didn't go happily. In addition to all the confusion and grief and sleeplessness I carried
with me, now I carried resentment, too.

Even so, I didn't yet have the confidence or clarity required
to leave, and I stayed for five more exhausting years. When baby
Josie was six months old, I requested to go "part time." This was a
big, hairy deal at the firm back then; only a couple other women
had done it previously. My part-time schedule looked like this:
four ten-hour days in the office, Monday through Thursday,
with Fridays technically "off"—with the caveat that I would
need to be available to clients and colleagues as they needed, and
that my absence would be invisible both inside and outside the
company. Feeling choiceless, I agreed—and took a 20 percent
pay cut for the privilege. And those "off" days were exactly what
you'd expect from a firm where the unofficial motto was: "We
don't take vacations so our clients can."

Things only got crazier when our second child, Julia, was
born two years later. Too often through my daughters' infant
and toddler years, I was the first parent to drop off at our YMCA's
childcare center *and* the last one to pick them up in the evening.
In the short winter months, this meant going to daycare in the
dark and going home in the dark, too. Knowing they'd charge
a buck a minute if I showed up after the 6 p.m. pickup dead-
line motivated me to hustle out of the actual office but I was
most certainly still working as we drove home: shushing my little

ones, who just needed their mama after their own long day, so I could reassure testy clients. How completely backwards! Then, once home, I wasn't actually *there,* either, firing up the laptop and yakking on Ye Olde Flip Phone. Thank God my husband had a less demanding schedule at the time and liked to cook, because kids can't eat conference calls.

After dinner, like so many working parents, I'd rush distracted through the bath/book/bed routine only to get back on the computer for a couple more hours. I wish I could slow down the playback of those memories and catch a glimpse of myself in love with the moment, with the simple joy of gently leaning my daughter's head back under the faucet to rinse the sudsy No More Tears from her curly blond mop. Sadly, that's not what I see when I replay that old tape. Instead, I see a harried, scattered, impatient, resentful woman who was unhappy at work and unhappy at home—because the demands of both at the same time made each one unenjoyable.

The thrill of ambitious overachieving turned into the heavy weight of overwhelming responsibility, and alcohol was the only way I knew how to turn off the chaos in my brain.

I'd always been a drinker, in the same way that I had always been sassy or funny: it was simply part of my identity, the way I moved through the world. My first drink and my first drunk came at the same time, at age twelve, the night of my mom's fortieth birthday party. While the adults celebrated, a school friend and I had our own party with a box of Franzia and a pan of brownies (a most unfortunate pairing, I must say). I remember vividly crawling up the basement steps to the first floor, then up another flight to the bathroom where the porcelain throne and I first became acquainted. The next morning, a Sunday, I got my first taste of "deadlines despite hangovers," powering through to finish a social studies paper on the Oregon Trail. Per usual, I got an A.

Alcohol was no stranger in my childhood home. My dad drank Budweiser for breakfast and Chivas at eleven o'clock in the morning, and I don't know what he had for lunch but I'm fairly certain it wasn't food. Drinking for him—and, later, for me—was as natural as breathing. After my parents split when I was fourteen, I stayed with my dad. I became his drinking buddy, and he became mine. In my high school years, it was Southern Comfort and grape juice before school and a long-neck Bud after. I can see only in retrospect, as the parent of a daughter that age, what a jarring, juxtaposed image I presented: a child clad in the red plaid skirt of her Catholic school uniform, with a beer bottle in one hand and a Marlboro in the other.

Through high school and college, I drank far more than my peers, and was a daily drinker by my early twenties. Talking with a friend on the phone one evening after work, I mentioned that I was watching TV and had just poured a glass of wine.

"You're not drinking alone, are you?" she asked worriedly.

"Of course not," I said. "The cats are here!"

By then I'd graduated to wine from a bottle, not a box. With every raise at work, my tastes and purchases leveled up a notch. I got into *Wine Spectator* ratings and studied the differences between a Napa Valley Cab and a Paso Robles Zinfandel. When my husband and I traveled to the Bahamas for our weeklong honeymoon, we packed three suitcases: one for him, one for me, and one that contained fifteen carefully wrapped bottles of wine. We drank every last one. It never occurred to me that this was unusual behavior.

By my thirties, that bottle-a-night habit wasn't reserved just for vacations or weekends; it became the necessary salve simply for living. I was a woman with two adorable children, a marriage that seemed rock-solid, a six-figure salary, and a kick-ass shoe collection—and here I was, drinking myself into oblivion, just like my dad used to. I did stupid things, too, just like he did, although my antics didn't involve regularly brandishing a weapon. (Though I do remember a particularly drunken holiday party soon after coming back to work from maternity leave, during which I pulled a milk-full breast out of my dress and squirted a male colleague across the bar. *Talk about an assault!* Facepalm.) While that one drew snickers, and still does to this day, not all the shenanigans were so harmless. I acted in ways that were inappropriate, illegal, and unsafe. I said horrible things to people. I was not to be trusted.

I can admit these things and tell those stories now without shame. Hell, I can even laugh at many of them. At the time, however, the staggering amount of anguish, embarrassment, remorse, and self-loathing that I carried obscured any light I could see in myself. No one was more disgusted by my behavior than me. Still, I couldn't stop, couldn't step back. So, I'd wake in the morning with a pounding head, pull myself together for another day at the office, and wrestle with the question that followed me around like Pigpen's stink cloud: *Who am I going to disappoint today?*

You can see that the problem, of course, wasn't actually the job. The problem was that I was living a life that looked good on the outside but felt horrible on the inside. The problem was that I was on autopilot, stuck in outdated priorities that weren't mine. The problem was that I ignored my own needs and desires, and instead set unrealistic expectations, projected my perfectionism onto other people, and offered very little in terms of patience or forgiveness. I wanted freedom but felt like I was in prison. The tension in my life always built but never released. As a result, I became a pressure cooker.

On the side of all the work and all the drinking, I was a devoted student of yoga who should have known better. I was such a devoted student, in fact, that I trained on nights and weekends to become a teacher, too. You might think that yoga's influence would have led me to listen more closely to my soul, and it did—*but not right away*. Until then, the best I could do was commiserate with friends until it became clear that my dissatisfaction was not unique; on the contrary, it was nearly universal. It seemed everyone secretly longed for a different way of living—whether that meant a different profession or a different relationship, even just a different way of relating to the world—but few were bold enough to chase it down. Those who did earned a standing ovation, while the rest of us just sat back and wondered whether we'd ever have the guts to shake up our existence.

Come On, It Isn't That Bad—or Is It?

In the early 1960s, marine biologist Rachel Carson wrote a book called *Silent Spring* that sparked an entire generation of environmentalists to action. Her topic was the damage to society caused by the slow consumption of pesticides, but I think her questions can apply equally to those in a state of "stuckness" today.

"Why should we tolerate a diet of weak poisons, a home in insipid surroundings, a circle of acquaintances who are not quite our enemies, the noise of motors with just enough relief to prevent insanity?" Carson wrote. "Who would want to live in a world which is just not quite fatal?"[1]

Not. Quite. Fatal.

Zing.

That's a space I lived in for years, thinking it was acceptable, somehow, because I knew it could have been worse, because other people *had* it worse. And who was I to want better when life wasn't great but it wasn't quite killing me, either?

Then I realized: when you're not quite dead, you're not quite alive, either.

I wrote this book to help anyone who feels trapped or choiceless become empowered to go after the life they most deeply desire.

But what if you don't know what that life looks like?

What if the life you have is *perfectly fine, thank you*—and yet something is . . . *missing*?

What if you feel like a greedy scumbag for wanting more?

What if you desperately want change but can't bear the idea of rocking the boat, or hurting someone's feelings, or leaving someone behind?

What if you feel like your discomfort, in comparison to so

many others' truly dire situations, isn't really *that* bad? And you ought to just suck it up and be grateful for what you've got?

What if you don't have the money or the time or the education or the support you need to chase your dreams? What if you're just barely keeping your head above water?

What if you're scared to death of being ridiculed for even trying? What if you stick your neck out only to have it broken?

What if the voice in your head—or voices outside of you—scream, repeatedly, that *you're not good enough, not smart enough, not special enough to have anything different*; that, in fact, *you're so utterly worthless that you barely deserve what you have now?*

Or what if you're just so damn numb, exhausted, dominated by pain, or lost in a hole so deep that you kind of want to give up?

First of all, let me assure you that you are not alone. Not by a long shot.

There are millions of people out there just like you—just like me—who crave a life that's somehow at odds with the one they are currently living. There are millions of us seeking an existence built on meaning, fulfillment, and freedom.

Even better, there are millions of people out there who have found that freedom and fulfillment. *Created it.* Just glance around and you'll see folks who were brave enough to make the changes they needed to build the life they longed for.

Consider the ones who quit their soul-sucking jobs and found something different . . . the ones who used to work for The Man and now work for themselves . . . the ones who used to numb life with booze or pills and now are clean and sober . . . the ones who mustered up the courage to leave an unhappy relationship in order to try again . . . the ones who overhauled an unhealthy lifestyle . . . the ones who moved mountains and miles to follow the song of their heart . . . the ones hurting enough to ask for help . . . the ones willing to face their trauma head on in order to heal body and soul.

I've taught hundreds of people just like this over the years in my workshops, retreats, and online courses. They didn't arrive in their new lives by accident; rather, they made hard and brave and necessary *choices*. You can, too.

This Book

We feel stuck when the life we're living doesn't line up with the life we want. We feel stuck when it seems like we don't have options. We feel stuck when we don't trust ourselves, or allow ourselves, to make the changes we so deeply long to make.

The truth is that every thought, every action, every reaction is a choice—you can stay put or move on, hold your tongue or speak up, get lost in the fear that keeps you believing the myth of "I can't" or get bold enough to find your way to yes. Even when the alternatives are "bad" and "worse," you still get to take your pick. We all *have* choices, and when we make them from a place of inner wisdom rather than fear, we create something powerful and true.

The journey we'll take in this book is one of soul excavation and action planning. It is divided into three sections to guide you first through understanding both the general phenomenon of "stuck" as well as your specific situation; then move you from fear to choice; and, finally, to taking confident action. Because, as the saying goes, nothing changes if nothing changes. This book will help you envision the life you most deeply desire, and then turn your intentions into real empowerment. If you follow the process all the way through, you'll end up with a playbook—created *for* you, and *by* you, not by some outside know-it-all—that reflects your values and priorities, your definition of success, and your individual life circumstances. Your plan of action will be as unique as your thumbprint.

The process I offer you involves nine steps:

1. Seeing the ways in which feeling stuck impacts your day-to-day life.
2. Articulating clearly, perhaps for the first time, what it is you *don't* want.
3. Understanding what you want instead, and why.
4. Facing squarely the fears that keep you stagnant.
5. Leveraging your divine inner badass and the other superpowers of a yoga mindset.
6. Deciding to make soul-guided choices.
7. Identifying the inevitable trade-offs, consequences, and boundaries you're likely to encounter.
8. Creating a strategic, detailed, personalized playbook to guide your next moves.
9. Integrating practices into your life that will bring ongoing care, grounding, healing, and peace for your journey.

A distinctive element of this book is that it's informed by my twenty years as a student and teacher of yoga. Before you get scared and run off, let me tell you what yoga is and what yoga isn't: Yoga is not a cult. It's not a religion. And you don't have to be able to stand on your hands or put your foot behind your head or capture any fancy poses on the beach at sunset for Instagram to participate in it. All you have to do, really, is breathe and allow the practice to introduce you to a new way of viewing yourself in the world.

Throughout this book I'll offer a modern take on some of the fundamental tenets of ancient yoga philosophy—such as impermanence, acceptance, and divinity—that can help you reset your priorities, drown out the naysaying voices in your head, and make bold choices in support of the life you desire. As Alexa Torontow writes in her poem "When We Get Quiet Enough":

When we get quiet enough
For long enough
We can hear the whispers
Of what is right
Of what is true
And most importantly
Which way is home.[2]

Write What You Know

There has long been a criticism that the field of self-help and personal development sidesteps the basic tension between inherent privilege and intersectionality, and to ignore this would be ridiculous. *Write what you know,* they say.

And, so, I'll tell you I write from the lived experience of a straight, married, white, able-bodied, college-educated woman who was raised Catholic (and later revolted against it), in the sprawled-out suburbs of St. Louis, Missouri. That means I do not know firsthand what it is like to be Black or Brown or Indigenous, or a man, or queer, or to struggle with fertility or chronic illness, or live in crushing poverty. I do not know firsthand what it's like to be discriminated against because of my ethnicity or financial status, the color of my skin or shape of my eyes, or the characteristics of the person I love. I do not know firsthand what it's truly like to not have a voice or a choice. Which means all the pain I do know may look really different than that of someone who knows, firsthand, a life that's different than mine.

I say this not to disqualify either my experience or my perspective, or their usefulness to others, but to acknowledge that I know what I can ably speak to and what I might just be guessing about. I write what I know and what I know is this: you deserve to live a life you dream of, not one you want to break free from but can't figure out how.

What's more, I know you can create this life if you so choose.

As you work through this book, please don't do it casually. Grab a journal and pen. Reflect deeply as you read. Scribble notes in the margins, put brackets around the sections you want to revisit, underline and asterisk and highlight until your hand falls off. Nothing short of utter defacement will make me happier.

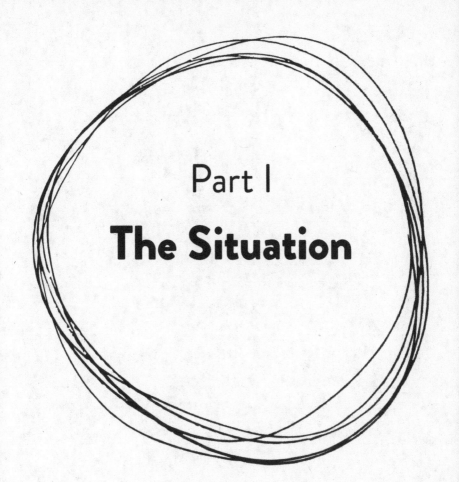

Part I
The Situation

1

The Empowerment Gap

If we stay where we are, where we're stuck, where we're comfortable and safe, we die there. We become like mushrooms, living in the dark, with poop up to our chins.
—**Anne Lamott**

The first step toward solving any problem is to understand it better: So, what exactly is "stuck" and how does it materialize in your day-to-day experience? What patterns have you fallen into that keep you from moving forward? What is your mindset about your situation and your capacity to change it?

For many, stuck feels like being confused by a complicated math question or overwhelmed by a ten-thousand-piece puzzle: stumped, stymied, unsure how to even approach it. In that sense, it's a mental block. Others feel it as a physical struggle in which you lose the battle every time you try to fight, like sinking deeper into quicksand when you move to get out, or spinning on tires that can't get traction.

I've known stuck more as an emotional state with real physiological elements: a sense of being trapped, cornered, boxed in, powerless, can't move left, can't move right. It's the breath I can't catch, like being alive in a coffin.

Take a pause here. How does "stuck" show up for you?

Whether it manifests as a mental, physical, or emotional state, feeling stuck is a wretched predicament, indeed. What begins as a single thought of dissatisfaction can become, over time, the way you perceive your lot in life and your options in the world. It can make you believe there are no viable alternatives and no way out. It can consume, like a cancer, taking root in one aspect of life—like a job, a relationship, a bad habit, or way of thinking—and spread its stranglehold to others. Left unchecked, a sense of stuck can steal your sense of freedom and render you stagnant.

If stuck is heavy, then its opposite is light: light on the bones, with light in the eyes, a garment worn loosely but that fits like an extra-supple second skin. Weightless, but with gravitas. Grounded. Centered. Clear. Knowing. (If unstuck were a voice, I'd like to think it belongs to Denzel Washington. I mean, can you *imagine* feeling stuck with Denzel murmuring in your ear?)

It's important to remember, especially when you're eyeball-deep in it, that stuck defines a feeling, a situation, a circumstance, or a season—but I do not ever, *ever,* apply it to a person or a life. You, as an individual, are not stuck, even if the muck you are sitting in feels thick and deep and self-generating. It is *not* your identity. The mire may be gluey and stagnant, but you are sovereign and powerful—exponentially more powerful than you may realize. You are a divine being with agency, ability, muscle, discernment, and, most notably, choice.

That choice is your greatest gift and your sharpest tool. It is your passage to freedom. It is *everything*.

Why Do We Stay Stuck?

When I finally decided to leave corporate America after five long years of exhausting mind-fucking and handwringing over whether I could actually go through with it, I felt like a damn superhero. Victorious! Unstoppable! I'm pretty sure I exited my boss's office after delivering the news in full strut mode, with more swagger than John Travolta in the opening credits of *Saturday Night Fever*. It was shocking, at least in my circles, that a rising star would quit unexpectedly—especially when there'd been no better-paying offer from a competitor, no huge falling-out with the big cheese, no major embarrassing screw-up. There was no reason other than *I wanted to*.

People reached out as the news made its way around the virtual watercooler. They spoke in wistful voices about wanting to do the same thing, offered the standard reasons for why they never could—*been doing this so long I don't know what I'd do instead, can't give up the paycheck, kids to put through college, etc.*—and gushed over how brave and admirable it was that I actually *did*. Surprisingly, some of the most heartfelt confessions came from senior male executives who had watched their wives and daughters struggle with many of the same questions I had, and who had struggled with them personally as well. I left every encounter feeling like a great and noble rebel, some counterculture hero.

But within a few months of settling into a new normal, the

shine of triumphant rebellion muted to thoughts of *Why hadn't I done this sooner?* Whole years had been lost—poof!—never to be reclaimed. All of a sudden, I didn't feel so brave, and my swagger was softened by a sense of regret that I hadn't grown a backbone earlier.

That got me wondering: What causes us to stay put in circumstances we hate when we could seemingly choose something else? I'm not referring only to jobs, of course, but to obviously unhealthy or toxic romantic relationships, friendships that suck us dry, or habits we know beyond doubt are making us miserable.

I had my theories about this but rather than simply guess at the answers, I decided to ask the questions. In 2015, I surveyed 550 people[1] online to better understand just how stuck people believe themselves to be, how that makes them feel, and what they do—or, importantly, don't do—in response. The results revealed a tension that surprised me. People see clearly the need to shift something big in their lives—in fact, many of them know *precisely* what needs to change—but one powerful force keeps them from initiating it: a perceived lack of license, an absence of agency, a poverty of permission.

This is what I call "the empowerment gap"—a sense of stuckness that comes from

> This is what I call "the empowerment gap"—a sense of stuckness that comes from a lack of feeling authorized to prioritize oneself, to take action, to change the status quo. It's a felt sense of being illegitimate in your own life, unsanctioned to take charge. But who better to sanction your own life than *you*?

a lack of feeling authorized to prioritize oneself, to take action, to change the status quo. It's a felt sense of being illegitimate in your own life, unsanctioned to take charge. But who better to sanction your own life than *you*?

Here's the thing—well, two things. First, feeling stuck is a natural human experience, especially in these modern times when there are so many systems in place to keep things humming in a very particular way. It's no longer the Wild West of self-determination when so much has been established: there are expectations for what you should do at every age, in alignment with cultural norms and religious traditions and political frameworks, inarguably influenced by entrenched perceptions on class and race and gender. It takes a ridiculous amount of guts to disrupt the status quo (or to even believe you can in the first place).

The second thing flows out of the first: pretty much everybody feels stuck at one stage or another, not just you. My research showed it's a universal phenomenon that spans gender, age, geography, income, education, and religion. In fact, virtually every survey respondent—98 percent—said they'd been stuck at some point.

The most common pain points?

- Professional dissatisfaction (60 percent)
- Relationships (51 percent)
- Personal habits/behaviors (49 percent)

Respondents reported the stagnation left them feeling:

- Sad and depressed (65 percent)
- Overwhelmed (58 percent)

- Helpless (44 percent)

And, in response, they reported doing what so many of us do:

- Withdraw (65 percent)
- Cry (48 percent)
- Procrastinate (46 percent)

Worse, they admitted they were more likely to deal with their feelings by turning to alcohol, drugs, or food than talking about solutions or making a plan for change.

The most intriguing numbers in the research are the ones that revealed "the empowerment gap": 62 percent of survey respondents said they *needed* to change, 43 percent said they were *ready* to change, but just 14 percent said they felt *empowered* to change.

That's right, only 14 percent. One in eight.

Any of this sound familiar?

Stuck Doesn't Discriminate

My study isn't the only one that speaks to this widespread dissatisfaction. A survey by GoDaddy[2] in 2016 found that two-thirds of Americans feel "stuck in a rut" in their personal and professional lives, and nearly a third confess that they lack the confidence and motivation to take a big risk. A 2017 survey by the Harris Poll[3] found only three out of ten Americans are happy; the 2015 UK Optimism Audit[4] told a similar story in Britain.

The pervasive sense of stuck doesn't discriminate—but the pressures underlying it seem to differ somewhat for men and women. Women, for example, have actually become *less* happy over the last three decades, even as wages, education, opportunity, and autonomy have risen. That's a trend consistent whether a woman works outside the home or stays in to raise kids, whether she's married or divorced, young or old, more or less educated.

This plays right into a theory that became evident in my thirties: the first generation of girls raised on the promise of "you can have it all" has grown up strung out on the pressure of trying to achieve an entirely unachievable standard. Of course women have become *less* happy! Opportunity has become an inescapable noose of expectations as the option to choose *anything* has morphed into an impossible mandate to undertake, and excel at, *everything*. Overwhelming doesn't begin to describe it.

> Opportunity has become an inescapable noose of expectations as the option to choose *anything* has morphed into an impossible mandate to undertake, and excel at, *everything*.

The women who came before me could not have predicted what unintended burdens their efforts would bear: a whole swath of society fighting an internal battle of ambition versus sanity, options versus the logical constraints of a twenty-four-hour day. It's no wonder one in eight Americans is on antidepressants—an increase of nearly 65 percent over fifteen years[5]—with women twice as likely to take them as men. And is it any surprise alcohol abuse among women in the U.S. is up nearly 84 percent[6] in the last decade? Today's "mommy juice" culture is literally dripping with women drinking to cope with their lives. (And the COVID-19 pandemic shot those rates even higher.)

Men have been struggling, too, amid job losses, tension over the American political divide, and societal expectations of what masculinity looks like, especially in an age where "patriarchy" is, understandably, a dirty word. The sense of marginalization and ostracization many men feel in the aftermath of #MeToo, the women's social justice movement that caught fire in 2017, is deep and often overlooked. As one friend observed to me: "Men feel just as trapped and vulnerable as women do. The difference is that men are cast as the villains in today's world; we are what is to be destroyed, not understood. This often leaves us to silently suffer—or at least feel like we are."

Men are three times more likely to commit suicide than women. White men, in fact, account for 70 percent of suicides in the U.S., noted Stephen Rodrick in an in-depth, A-plus piece of journalism for *Rolling Stone* titled "All-American Despair."[7] "The American white man," he wrote, "is responsible for enough suicides annually (more than 47,000 in 2017) that Madison Square Garden could not hold all the victims."

Of course, life is far more complex and multidimensional than that, making it unfair to categorize the experience as simply "male" or "female." Each individual experiences it from the intersection of multiple overlapping aspects of their circumstances and history. Gender is merely one: race, heritage, language, age, education, ability, socioeconomic status, sexual identity, political association, relationship to religion and spirituality, being a target of violence, and many other characteristics shape our experiences as well.

Years That Ask Questions, Years That Answer

Still, there is reason for optimism. In my survey, a hearty 75 percent of respondents said they believed their situation was changeable or their problem was solvable, and 60 percent said they had a clear vision for what they wanted their life to look like. "Free," "joyful," "purposeful," "unafraid," and "confident," were the ideals offered by most. (Just listen to Denzel whisper those words in your ear! They sound pretty nice, don't they?)

Then came the COVID-19 pandemic of 2020, and the world as many of us knew it ground to a frantic halt. Many of us hid inside our homes, in our soft pants—some of us by choice and some of us because the government mandated it. Our kids came home, too, as did their schooling. While an estimated 42 percent of the US workforce transitioned to working from home during the height of lockdown[8], millions of us still had to show up on the job site—in hospitals and supermarkets and daycare centers that hadn't closed—and we all tried, under excruciating circumstances, to juggle it all. "Joyful" and "free" became lofty ideals as our goals shifted to staying safe, alive, and—bonus!—remembering what day it was. "Normal" became a memory, and now became a time marked by stress and confusion, bitter frustration, loneliness, and grief. We slid into survival mode.

If there is *any* upside to a tragedy that has claimed, as of this writing, more than 6 million lives worldwide, and I do not say this lightly, it's that we have been forced to rethink what we value, prioritize, and perceive. We have been given the opportunity to be more intentional about what is reintroduced and how these elements work together in service of the whole person, the whole life, the whole society.

This forced recalibration shows us the value of asking questions in every aspect of life (something we'll explore more in Chapter 3). Perhaps you've found yourself pondering along these lines, too:

- **Relationships:** Where do I belong? What kinds of connections are most important? Which ones lift me up? Where can I let go?
- **Work:** Does my job fulfill me and, if not, what else might? What proportion of my energy and time should this receive? How do I achieve balance with the rest of my life?
- **Money:** Do I spend wisely? How might I earn money differently? How much is enough?
- **Time:** How much time do I have? Does the way I use my time reflect what's important to me?
- **Family:** What's working in my family structure, patterns, and relationships? What's not?
- **Faith and identity:** Who am I in this world? Who's got my back? What do I believe?
- **Health and well-being:** Am I avoiding any issues? Am I caring for myself sufficiently and in the right ways?

To get a better sense of what people were thinking as the COVID lifestyle transitioned into its next iteration, I put that

2015 survey back out into the field in mid-2021, adding some questions tied to the pandemic's impact. While not a scientific piece of research, the responses showed some clear trends:

- Folks feel as stuck and overwhelmed as ever.
- Habits and coping mechanisms edged out jobs as the number-one area where people want to create change.
- Improving physical and mental health, and rethinking how they spend their time, emerged as high priorities.
- While 28 percent said they were eager to "get back to normal," 37 percent said they were excited to "create a new normal."

That sense of sovereignty and agency pulled through in other questions, as well. Most notably, in the first survey, only 14 percent said they felt empowered to change things that weren't working in their lives. But, coming out of the pandemic, 42 percent reported they felt *more empowered* to change! That's a telling shift (or, as I like to say, a *Big Fucking Deal*): four out of ten people looked squarely at a year of fear, chaos, and uncertainty, and, rather than buckling under it or acquiescing to it, emerged with a greater knowledge that they can—they *must*—take ownership over their own lives.

Are you one of them? Are you hearing a voice inside of you screaming, *Enough! I can't take it anymore!* and you know that change can't wait? Are you, as we say in 12-step programs, sick and tired of feeling sick and tired?

Good. Be honest about where it hurts, and let's do something about it.

Closing Exercise:
You Are Not Stuck Survey

Following are the eight questions I first posed to folks in 2015. This is your starting point. While the questions themselves are simple, they provoke a deep look within. Answer these questions to better understand what you do, or don't do; when you're feeling stuck; how it shows up in broad patterns and specific behaviors; and how all that makes you feel inside. Gathering this important information is the first step in your journey toward change.

1. Do you feel stuck from time to time?

Yes

No

I don't know

2. In what area(s) of your life do you feel the *most* stuck? (Please select up to three.)

Relationship

Job/career

Children

Family

Finances

Health/body

Mental health/outlook

Habits/behavior patterns

Other _____

3. How do you feel about being stuck? (Please select all that apply.)

   Sad/depressed

   Hopeless/no way out

   Scared

   Angry

   Overwhelmed

   Apathetic

   Bitter/resentful

   Need to change

   Ready to change

   Empowered to change

   Other _____

4. What do you do when you feel stuck? (Please select all that apply.)

   Become angry/act aggressively

   Become sad/cry

   Complain

   Withdraw

   Procrastinate

   Avoid completely

   Engage in healthy behavior (e.g. exercise, meditate, get a massage)

   Engage in unhealthy behavior (e.g. alcohol, drugs, overeating)

   Talk about solutions/make a plan

   Nothing/I'm immobilized

   Other _____

5. Do you believe your situation/problem is changeable/solvable?

    Yes

    No

    I don't know

6. Do you have a vision for what the life you want looks/feels like?

    Yes

    No

    I don't know

    If "yes," please elaborate: _____

    _____

7. Do you know what specific changes need to be made to achieve that vision?

    Yes

    No

    I don't know

    If "yes," please elaborate: _____

    _____

8. What specifically do you feel is standing in the way of creating the life you want? (Please select all that apply.)

    Fear of failure

    Fear of criticism/ridicule

    Fear of change/the unknown

    Starting over

Lack of money/financial considerations
Lack of support from spouse/family/friends
Don't know how
The effort/work required to learn/do new things
Don't believe I can achieve it
Don't feel I deserve it
Other _____

Allow a pause here. Look back at your answers and what they say about your current state of "stuckness." Within your responses to those eight simple questions lie significant clues about what's not working in your life and what may need to change. Honor what the clues tell you and how they make you feel, without any judgment about whether you think you *should* feel that way. This journey begins with listening to your gut.

Indigestion of Shoulds

There are two ways you can live: you can devote your life to staying in your comfort zone, or you can work on your freedom.
—**Michael Singer**

There is a line in one of my favorite books, *Emotional Sobriety* by Tian Dayton,[1] that I haven't forgotten since the moment I saw it: "Normal is anything you're used to."

Notice she doesn't say "normal is the way it's supposed to be" or "normal is good" or "normal is nothing to complain about" . . . but normal is simply anything to which you've become accustomed. (Think paying three dollars for a bottle of water or texting your kids when they're in the next room or no longer being able to see your eyebrows to pluck them.)

Truth is, we humans can get used to some pretty crazy things: pineapple on pizza, prescription drug commercials on TV, the latest slang, active shooter drills in our kids' schools. Look at the way the COVID pandemic normalized widespread, prolonged mask wearing and social distancing and homeschooling and, for a time, wiping down our groceries—all things we never could have predicted but got used to fairly quickly. Then, once the majority of people began receiving vaccines (at least in developed nations) and restrictions loosened, many of us became anxious about *not* wearing masks and social distancing and the rest of it.

Normal is anything you're used to.

This happens in almost every aspect of life, especially in areas where the stakes are highest, where we invest ourselves the most, and expect the biggest return on that investment. And, not surprisingly, it happens often in those areas that people say they feel most stuck: jobs, relationships, habits, and coping mechanisms.

Consider a relationship as an example, whether a romantic partnership or a close friendship. It starts off steamy. The connection is there. You talk and talk, feel seen and understood, your walls come down. Familiarity gives way to real intimacy. Then, one day, you notice some sense of distance that you can't quite identify. But it's real. It takes up space between you. Slowly, one of you pulls back. Then the other. You talk less, share less. It begins to feel normal because you've gotten used to it. *That's just the way it is.* And back and forth you go, stepping away one tiny step at a time, until that little bit of distance becomes a great chasm.

Or consider one of the ways you might wind down after a stressful nine-to-five (which sometimes feels more like a wake-to-sleep cycle these days, doesn't it?): a glass of wine to help smooth out the day's rough edges.

If the edges feel extra sharp, one glass might become two; or two, a bottle. And if stress levels are prolonged, perhaps the occasional evening drink becomes a string of them, with weeks turning into months and the desire to numb growing stronger than your perceived ability to manage the stress with a clear head. Maybe the pour begins earlier in the day, maybe wine gives way to something stronger.

Normal is anything you're used to.

Sounding the Alarm on Creeping Normality

Maybe drinking isn't your thing. Maybe it's eating crap food or smoking weed or phone scrolling into oblivion; or staying in a job that you can feel is sucking the best parts of you dry, or a relationship that is no longer satisfying or healthy; or a way of moving through the world that is keeping you scared or small when, truth is, you are anything but.

Perhaps you are fully aware of how bad things have gotten. More likely, though, the changes have been so gradual, almost imperceptible, that recognition of your new normal catches you off guard.

Experts call that "creeping normality." You can apply it not just to behaviors and circumstances, but how you think, how you're treated, how boundaries and nonnegotiables become eroded over time, how something once unacceptable can normalize into the status quo. A little becomes a lot, an inch becomes a mile, foreign becomes familiar, a death of a thousand cuts. Things seem *normal* until you understand they aren't. Habits work until they don't. Situations are tolerable until they're not.

I've hit this particular brick wall—the one spray-painted with big, bold words that read: "NOT THIS." You probably have, too. In fact, you may be looking at that wall this very moment.

The good news is that your body and mind aren't typically subtle in sounding the alarm when some aspect of life is terribly off-kilter. They will tell you, often quite loudly, using messengers such as insomnia, headaches, gut trouble, or constipation, as well as feelings of powerlessness, anger, high anxiety, deep desperation, or all-encompassing depression.

Trouble is, you're a busy person and not always in the frame of mind to slow down and listen. You've got things to do, what with the job and the family and the bills and whatnot, not to mention the notion of caring for yourself in the elusive thing known as "spare time." Or maybe you land on the low side of emotional fluency, so even if the warning bells are sounding, you may not recognize what you're hearing. Regardless, it's quite inconvenient when the deepest parts of you rise up in anguish, particularly when they speak in a language that you may struggle to interpret.

An inner uprising is agonizing to endure. To cope, you may elect to ignore it until it quiets down, responding to what initially presents as low-level discontent with behaviors to distract from what is troublesome. And because you are distracted, you may not notice the full scope of the problem until it has become so big that major intervention or change is in order. By then, you might be gearing up for the fight of your life, ready to run like hell, or with your feet frozen to the ground beneath you because the whole thing is just too overwhelming.

Perhaps that is where you are now; perhaps that's the state you are trying to avoid. Either way, you've got to listen to the

> To look away, to abandon yourself at this moment, could be the greatest tragedy of your life.

voice within shouting, "Not this," because to look away, to abandon yourself at this moment, could be the greatest tragedy of your life.

When Your Inner Knowing Won't Be Silenced

The phrase "not this" became part of my vernacular the instant I read Elizabeth Gilbert's essay[2] by that name in 2016. (If you've read it, too, you know what I mean; if you haven't, pause here and get to Google, stat. I'll wait.)

I remember the moment vividly: visiting a friend on the East coast, riding shotgun and scrolling Facebook while she drove, heart tight in my throat as I read the piece aloud to her. "Some deep life force within you is saying, NOT THIS," Liz wrote, "and it won't be silenced."

I knew that feeling because I was living it.

My twelve-year marriage had fallen apart the year before suddenly, unexpectedly, when I heard the words, "I'm sorry, I just don't love you anymore—and I haven't for quite some time." It was an immediate, searing heartbreak that exploded quickly into a fury that would take up residence in my chest for literal years.

"I had children with you," I hissed, as the sense of security I'd craved since childhood dissolved.

My instinct in that moment was to slam the door and run

and howl until I was empty of pain, but in an effort to keep the family intact for the sake of my daughters, who were then just seven and five, I stayed. Dave and I went to therapy. I nurtured my sobriety, which was then so tender and fresh, only a year old, and didn't drink. Still, I felt like life was happening *to me* rather than *because of me*.

During the months I wrestled with the decision of what to do next, I was miserable and every part of me knew it, even if I refused to say it out loud or even acknowledge it to myself. (Or, to be more accurate, I was miserable *because* I refused to say it out loud or acknowledge it to myself.) It was an agonizing stay in a painful purgatory. I was collateral damage as the certainty within me and the uncertainty around me fought an epic battle for my future, for my very soul.

Each day for weeks and months I asked my deepest wisdom if she knew yet what the next right step was. I was so conflicted because I desperately didn't want to give up prematurely or rob my girls of one of the things I value most—stability—but I also wouldn't, I couldn't, surrender to a marriage that suffered from a lack of love.

For the longest time, my deepest wisdom told me she didn't yet know. So, we kept processing. But when that essay placed onto my tongue the words my soul had been trying to speak— "not this"—I realized she knew, and with crystal clarity. Turns out Dave's wisdom knew it, too, so we agreed it was time to rip off the Band-Aid and move together toward being apart.

Wants Versus Shoulds

Only in retrospect can I understand that part of the reason I was so paralyzed during the months leading up to our decision to divorce was because I'd been trying to tackle the problem the wrong way. First, I was staring at it in its entirety, in all its complexity, rather than breaking it down into the smaller and simpler chunks that a human brain can more readily process. I was also trying to predict too far into the future where I had little to no control, rather than drawing my focus closer in on what I could manage in the moment. Even more, I was thinking of the impact such a decision would have on everyone but me. This all left me wailing, "Not this! Not this!" over and over but taking no steps that would guide me to clarity or action.

Most consequentially, though, I was living in the question of what *should be* rather than what *was,* what I thought I *should do* rather than what I *wanted.*

Researchers have long held that the inner battle between what you *want to do* versus what you *believe you should do* creates deep conflict that comes into play in decision-making. In the late eighties, psychologist E. Tory Higgins introduced self-discrepancy theory, which involves an individual's "ideal self" (which represents hopes and dreams) and an "ought self" (which is informed by a sense of roles, duties, and responsibilities). In the late nineties, Harvard Business School professor Max H. Bazerman dubbed this inner conflict a tension between the "want self" and the "should self."

Higgins's theory suggests it is not just the difference between the "ideal self" and the "ought self" that creates a problem, but rather the comparison of ideal or ought against the reality of one's actual life. Then, depending on the nature of the discrepancy, Higgins said it can trigger specific emotions that he put into two camps: dejection-related emotions (including disappointment, dissatisfaction, sadness, and frustration from unfulfilled desires) and agitation-related emotions (such as fear, edginess, restlessness, resentment, guilt, and self-contempt). People struggling with these inner conflicts often feel a sense of failure, unworthiness, or ineffectiveness and tend toward procrastination and

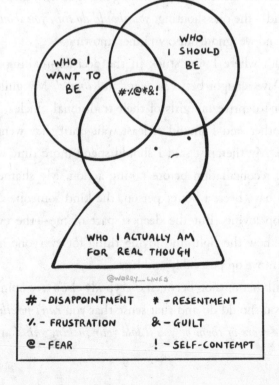

WHO I WANT TO BE

WHO I SHOULD BE

#%.@*&!

WHO I ACTUALLY AM FOR REAL THOUGH

@WORRY_LINES

# – DISAPPOINTMENT	* – RESENTMENT
%. – FRUSTRATION	& – GUILT
@ – FEAR	! – SELF-CONTEMPT

avoidance, he said, and, ultimately, the frustration of unfulfilled desires leads to depression and anxiety.

The tension between "want self" versus "should self," or the gap between "ideal" or "ought" and one's current self, can get exacerbated when a voice important to you—such as a spouse, parent, boss, or sibling—weighs in with what *they* think you should do. Of course, this applies not just to individuals but to peer groups like neighbors or friends, institutions such as government or church, or simply culture at large; *everybody* wants to give you their two goddamn cents! And, because we live in a society that values conformity over free and individual thinking, we find ourselves agonizing over, and often acquiescing to, Other People's opinions. We get stuck in exhausting dialogue with their voice in our head—the one shouting, *you should do this, you shouldn't do that*—and we ignore our own inner knowing.

That's where I was stuck in the decision-making process with Dave, caught between *want* and *should*. My guilt said I shouldn't deprive my girls of their traditional, nuclear family. My mother said I should at least wait until they went off to college. My therapist said I should spend more time working toward reconciliation before taking action. My shame said I should have been a better person, the kind someone couldn't just stop loving. But the deepest part of me—the ever-wise part—knew the right and loving thing for everyone involved was to move on peaceably and leave.

I call that tension between everybody else's free opinions on what you should do and that sense that you *can't possibly swallow one more of them or you'll lose your fucking mind* an "indigestion of shoulds." You are quite literally up to here with it and have reached the point where there are just two options: you can keep swallowing, or you can spit out all those extraneous, immaterial opinions and decide to honor the wisdom of your intuition and your soul.

When the voices of Other People drown out the voice of your own intuition, you exist in a state that's out of alignment, beyond your boundaries, and inconsistent with what your soul knows is right and true for you. Instead of natural, easy alignment between what you desire and how you're living, that "indigestion of shoulds" leaves you spending more time trying to beat back the discomfort in your chest than cultivating your freedom—until, that is, the voice of ignored pain turns into a primal scream.

You might experience that scream as a meltdown, a breakdown, a rock bottom. (I have experienced it as all of these and then some.) My hope is that it takes only one or two instances of this for you to recognize when something is Seriously Wrong—but, fact is, we humans can be pretty dense, and sometimes it takes more than one whack upside the proverbial head with a frying pan to get our attention.

Here's the lesson in a nutshell: Any failure to live up to someone else's expectation of you is a disappointment from which they *will* recover. But failure to live up to your own is a desertion of your very soul.

Any failure to live up to someone else's expectation of you is a disappointment from which they *will* recover. But failure to live up to your own is a desertion of your very soul.

What's Causing Your Indigestion?

We don't all have the same "not this." What causes heartburn in me might be just fine for you. And that's to be expected: we are vastly different people, with different upbringings, different experiences, different hang-ups, different boundaries.

While there are a number of fairly common sources of emotional indigestion, there can be a great deal of subjectivity, too. Something that is a "Hell, no!" for me may be a "God, yes!" for you. (Like fish, perhaps, or death metal.) And you may not think you have one right now, but if you are reading this book, I'd bet my dog there is something troubling you deeply—even if you refuse to name it, even if you don't know what name you'd place on it. It's there, gnawing on you, and it won't go away.

Let your mind wander over some examples less frightening than the ones I've shared so far. Take a practice run with naming a few things you absolutely can't live with, or without. For me, things like teaching kindergarten, living in a noisy city center, or working in a casino or on a construction site would all qualify as nonstarters; I'm simply too sound-sensitive. I can't stand tight spaces with lots of people, so you're not likely to find me on a cruise ship or in a crowded group exercise class. I don't do small talk or booze anymore, so count me out for happy hour. (And, just so we're clear, I wasn't kidding about the fish.)

Some folks' "not this" can seem counterintuitive or unexpected: the brilliant friend who quits the Ivy League school, the ambitious woman who passes on the once-in-a-lifetime job opportunity, the talented actor who retires at what appears to be the peak of his career. Britain's Prince Harry, who famously walked away from a seemingly fairy-tale life in the royal family, is proof that it's not about the way something appears from the outside, but rather how it feels on the inside.

Outsiders never know the full story, and insiders are under no obligation to explain themselves. Neither, my friend, are you. The important thing is that you learn to listen to the signals in your mind and body when it wants you to reject something, because one of the keys to knowing what you want is to understand, marrow-deep, what you don't.

Before I began implementing the principles I'll detail in the chapters ahead, I was stuck in a pattern that required situations to become so untenable, so terrible and desperate and rock-bottom low, for me to actually do something about them. This happened in my job, in my marriage, and in my drinking. What I've learned since is that circumstances don't need to get *that* bad, because "rock bottom" is relative and so much of the suffering we experience can be avoided when we live in a manner that brings our values, priorities, thoughts, words, and actions into better alignment.

That shift begins with acknowledging where your indigestion comes from. You can start by saying it aloud to no one but yourself or write it down in a secret place where no one will see. What's important is that you get radically honest about what's not working in your life. Once you are in more open, regular communication with your deeper being—when you are better attuned to what your body is telling you when you can't sleep, can't poop, can't make this headache go away, and you come to believe that your deepest needs and desires matter a great deal—you can recognize much earlier the signs of your "not this."

A word of caution here: Articulating what gives you the indigestion of shoulds often brings on a sense of deep despair. This is natural considering the gravity of the circumstances. But please don't despair for long because this can be a fateful moment. Saying "not this!" is more than an empty declaration; it represents the riverhead of essential, soul-excavating questions that will lead you home. The realization is a gift, and the work you'll do in the next chapters will help you unwrap that gift and use it as the springboard for understanding two key things: first, the "why" behind your "not this," and, second, what you want instead.

Bottom line: Change starts with acknowledging that the life you're living doesn't line up with the life you want. And it is never too late to change direction.

Closing Exercise: *Name the Problem*

What is the "indigestion of shoulds" or "not this" you're facing right now? In what area(s) of life are you feeling the most stuck, and why? If you're feeling more of a general unhappiness that doesn't seem to have a well-defined cause, be willing to dig here. Root around. Poke at things you can't yet see clearly and see what happens. I suspect you'll strike a rich vein before too long.

Once you do, let it all come up. Be as ruthlessly honest as you can, scribble as quickly as you can. This isn't about answers, this is about *feelings*. Hold nothing back and don't edit as you go, for this excavation is what sets you in the right direction.

3

Know What You Want Instead

The panther that has stalked you
*   since you were a child*
*   is old now. No longer wild,*
*   and tired of guarding the treasure*
*   you yourself left behind—*
*   blind and deaf, she will give it all to you*
*   if you just let her go.*
—Pat Schneider

The first step in moving away from the life you feel stuck in and getting closer to the one you dream of is to name what you *don't* want—your "not this"—whatever it is that robs you of peace, that makes you feel like unused potential, that makes you gnash your teeth in anguish and wonder: *What is the freakin' point?*

The next step is to identify what you *do.*

Getting clear on what that looks like isn't a particularly easy endeavor, of course; if it were, I could have made this a two-chapter book, tacked on a "P.S." at the end, and called it a day. It involves a significant amount of deep and sometimes difficult work—but I'll tell you it may just be the most consequential, rewarding work you'll ever do.

There lies in front of you a rich field just waiting to be excavated, a treasure of archaeological clues that will help you piece together your future from your past. This is the ground from which the calling of your soul can spring up and take shape. Not only will you find the digging in this dirt informative, it is emotive, too. There are facts *and* feelings to discover here, which means you can consider your path to soul-guided choices not only from the single dimension of your intellectual headspace, but with the holistic power of your mind, spirit, and body wisdom. And, trust me, the sum of these parts is so much greater than any one of them on their own.

The lament I hear most often from people in my workshops is: "I just don't know who I'm supposed to be." At least half the time that comes up in the context of profession or purpose, but it also relates to family roles, the quest for spirituality, and the essence of your innermost truth.

Should I be an accountant or a painter?

Should I stay home with my kids or work outside the home?

How passionate or outspoken or rebellious can I get away with being?

Am I supposed to lead or follow, inspire or be inspired, take orders or give them, create or consume other people's creations?

To whom am I most obligated—my parents, my partner, my deeper self?

What is my purpose on this earth?

So, when someone says, "I just don't know who I'm supposed to be," my response comes back first in the form of a question—"Who do you *want* to be?"—then, advice as sung by The Avett Brothers: "Decide what to be and go be it."[1]

That's the crux of this whole ballgame: you get to curate a life experience of your own choosing. That experience is influenced, of course, by some circumstances beyond your control—the genes you inherited, the nature and culture of your family of origin, the physical and social and financial space you were born into—but at some point, your existence becomes a culmination of the choices you make or don't make.

It's natural to consider the "sunk costs" of the choices you've made thus far—time or money or energy you've already invested into whatever it is that's got you feeling stuck, resources you can't ever recoup. *Welp, there's ten years I'll never get back!* But truth is, it is never too late to realize the path you've been walking isn't the one you want to keep walking. You have the permission, the ability, the *responsibility* to course correct when you need to—the only other element required is the guts.

And, remember, a decision to change course doesn't imply that the direction you've been headed all this time was the wrong one—perhaps it served you well for years and years—

and, bonus, it brought you to the place where you stand today: wiser, more connected to your evolving spirit, and ready for something different. That's not failure, that's awakening.

The question is, awakening to *what?*

Contrast and South Stars

The first place to look for information is in the gut reactions to where you find yourself now versus where you wish to be instead. Those reactions can point you in a direction, however vague that initial direction may be. (It's like what E. L. Doctorow said about writing: "Writing is like driving at night in the fog. You can only see as far as your headlights, but you can make the whole trip that way."[2]) Your understanding of yourself works that way, too. You collect one fuzzy learning, and then another, and another until they begin to pile up and amount to something big on the horizon, a hazy shape that comes into clearer focus as you get closer to it.

The investigation into that rich realm between what you don't want and what you do is more involved than a leap from one opposite to another; it's not as simple as: "I don't want white so I must want black." Yet contrast is an excellent teacher, because to explore contrast is to sit with complexity, and complexity forces us to get familiar with nuance. In that way, we become more astute and discerning than what simply black/white, either/or can allow for, and we begin to deal in shades. Not only shades of gray, either, but all aspects of the technicolor life ahead: warm and cool, energizing and calming, heady and sensual, strong and tender, whirring and still. In the study of contrast, we invite all of the colors and all their variations in every level of opacity and translucence. Then, with the benefit of that full spectrum of vision, we can better evaluate and pinpoint our preferences.

Consider the gut sense that arises when you ponder the difference between opposing ideas such as tight and spacious . . . empty and brimming . . . before and after . . . false and true . . . blind and seeing . . . forcing and allowing. If your response is anything like mine, there is more than a quick right/wrong, good/evil response. These words, especially when set up against their flip side, also conjure up emotions, desires, and disappointments—weighted, too, with memory and meaning. It's in this space you can find deep insight into what you desire, what you don't, and why.

Rob Bell, the author and former pastor, refers to the recognition of the things we don't want as "south stars": "A south star is something that guides you because it's upside down, because it's backwards, because it's the opposite,"[3] he said on his podcast.

South stars illuminate and remind you of what you don't like, the kind of person you don't want to be, the way you refuse to exist in the world. They are the antithesis of your values, what you stand for. But the real value of a south star, like most opportunities for transformation, exists beyond the simple recognition of it. Conversion of a negative into a positive comes with action, so what you *do* with a south star is much more consequential than merely what you *think* of it.

Let me offer an example from my life. One of my south stars is pretending—pretending to be okay when you're anything but; pretending to be blind to or unbothered by things that are legitimately bothersome; pretending to be something or some-one you're just not. Each of these is a form of inauthenticity.

I can usually detect these bluffs and pretenses in others fairly easily (all those years as a journalist helped to fine-tune my inner bullshit meter). I didn't always recognize this behav-ior in myself, though, because pretending often masquerades as reflexively minimizing the importance of an issue or putting on one's so-called big-girl panties to just deal with it.

Over the years I have knowingly—and, more often, unknowingly—pretended myself into some pretty uncomfort-able predicaments. I stayed silent when I should have spoken up; I overextended myself for a prolonged period of time in a way that jeopardized my mental health.

But once I identified pretending as a south star, I began to consciously choose its opposite as a life principle. Now, in most cases, I focus on simply being who I am, as I am. I am guided by the desire to be genuine. On the occasion that I show up in a way that's not genuine, or must engage with someone else who is pretending, I feel the falseness down to my cells. And it hurts.

It hurts in the brain, hurts in the heart, hurts in the body. I've learned to listen to this discomfort, put the name on it, and then recalibrate to get back to my guiding value of authenticity. I don't beat myself up when this happens, I'm just grateful for the reminder to get back on track. (It's like the lane assist tech-nology in your car that will beep or shake your steering wheel if you veer out of your lane.) Paying attention to south stars is more important than you realize; that one gentle correction can make the difference between staying on the path and colliding with the end of you.

Values

If a south star points you to what you don't desire, a north star leads you to what you do. Think of a north star as a beacon, a signal fire, a touchstone—anything that reminds you which way is home in your heart. These are your values, guiding principles, rules to live by, what you stand for—and whatever you call them, they are the basis for your thoughts, beliefs, and actions.

Early on, most of us simply accept the values of others: When we are born into our families of origin, we also are born into the family's value system; when we go to school, we become influenced by the values of the institution; in the workplace, we are led by what the company holds as dear; if we partner up, we'll have to reckon with the other person's accumulated values, which stretch all the way back to *their* family of origin. If you belong to a community of any kind—a church, a neighborhood, team, fraternity, recovery program—you are impacted by those values as well.

While values represent an important foundation for the person you are, you are not set in them like posts in concrete. Like anything else that evolves, values must develop along with you if they are to be healthy and meaningful. You can outgrow a value in the same way you can outgrow a bra: one day it fits, at some point later you notice it's a little uncomfortable, then suddenly you realize you can't take a breath. What was designed to support you is now only serving to constrict. You're trying to breathe in a 32A when you've matured into a 38D.

My own values have evolved greatly over time. My twenties and early thirties were all about career building. I valued achievement, recognition, and upward mobility. I worked my ass off and wanted to be acknowledged for it, especially in the ways people couldn't help but notice: nice car, four-inch power heels, that sweet little title on my business card. The BMW I treated myself to when I turned thirty was a deliberate show of status, a message to the higher-ups: *Look, I'm a grownup, just like you! Let me into the club!* It was about me, me, and only *me*.

Slowly, though, some of the bits of wisdom I'd heard in the yoga classes I'd been taking for the last few years had sneaked in when I wasn't paying attention—or rather, they seeped in when I was paying attention to something other than work. When I slowed down enough and got quiet enough, a small voice inside would ask: *Are you throwing all your energy into the right thing? Isn't there more to this life than climbing, climbing, climbing that interminable fucking ladder?*

As I looked at the people standing on the rungs above me, still in the midst of their own climb, what struck me is that they didn't look any happier the higher they got. Actually, they just looked *more* miserable! I wanted absolutely zero part of more stress; I was already neck-deep in it and not coping particularly well.

Beyond my drinking, these years also held my first experiences with depression and its hallmark expression of frequent, uncontrollable tears.

There was the paralyzing anxiety that would come on during social settings like dinner at a friend's house or a birthday gathering at a bar and send me scrambling for that safe space behind the locked bathroom door. Once there, I'd crumple into more crying or just stare at my mirrored image, sad and ashamed that I couldn't control myself any better.

There were the mornings I found myself—coat on, keys in hand, computer bag slung over my shoulder for work—standing in front of the fridge, shoveling Ben & Jerry's into my face to numb out the smothering dread.

There was the afternoon I sobbed to my boss that I had thoughts of jumping out my nineteenth-story office window or ramming my car into a brick wall to get out of going to a client meeting that night.

There was the terrifying, unexpected panic attack on my way to a client meeting that left me immobilized and sobbing on a downtown corner. I had to be helped off the street and was sent, immediately and for the first time, to a therapist's office.

Believe it or not, none of this was visible to anyone else. (Or perhaps they were doing their own pretending?) All they saw was what I wanted them to see: a rising star who could handle anything that got thrown at her. I guess I can't blame them for throwing, eh?

After my girls were born, my values became much more family-centered: Everything was about home, time, togetherness. Because it was no longer all about me; it was about *them*. My signature need to be in the spotlight yielded to an instinct that was completely other-focused and therefore incredibly perplexing: *Wait! I thought I was the center of attention. How did these crying, pooping blobs become my entire universe?* Every action, every decision got filtered through the question of how it would enrich or entertain my children, and all I wanted was to be present enough to create savor-worthy moments and memories. I wanted to be there *for* my daughters, *with* them.

So, at thirty-eight, when they were a precious five and three,

I said goodbye to that job. I dove headlong—gleefully—into a second, more in-depth yoga teacher training. I gave birth to the You Are Not Stuck Facebook community and then I finally, miraculously, stopped drinking. (That's a Whole 'Nother Topic, which we'll cover in Chapter 6.) I felt happy and free and, for the first time in a long time, in charge of my own destiny.

Until, that is, the fateful day a year later when my marriage unexpectedly fell apart.

Time stopped then and, for the first time in possibly forever, so did I.

Depression chained me to the bed.

But as I started over, I stood on the values of truth and courage and spirituality and revival—my *north stars*—and began to measure success in the quality of my connection with other people, the depth of feeling and understanding and sharing.

Because, I realized, it's about *all of us*.

With sobriety and renewal as the springboard, my forties ushered in a return to self: not to the ego but the spiritual aspect of me I had been flirting with since my feet first stepped onto the yoga mat all those years before. It was a time of equal parts demolition and reconstruction, like taking a bathroom down to the studs before you make it all shiny with new plumbing, new electrical, new fixtures. Rabid self-sufficiency gave way to learning how to ask for help; arrogance grew into humility; my ever-present "game face" softened; and slowly I got good at telling the truth about how I felt and what I needed, even if sometimes I was telling no one other than myself. I became less afraid of the depression that came and went and came back again, and more compassionate toward it. I embraced myself as a glorious little disaster who is ridiculously imperfect but willing to grow.

I still am willing. I hope to die willing.

What Are Your Values?

If there's one thing I wish someone had told me when I was younger it's that lines are not meant to be toed, they are meant to be moved and redrawn and colored in and erased until they suit you—and you can do that as many times as you like.

> Lines are not meant to be toed, they are meant to be moved and redrawn and colored in and erased until they suit you—and you can do that as many times as you like. They're *your* lines, after all.

They're *your* lines, after all.

You are not intended to spend this life squeezed and choked and squashed in a vise of Other People's design, or values that aren't your own, or an outdated world view; no, you were made for discernment, cultivation, and expansion.

Until you realize that the internal forces that guide you will evolve as you do, and that you have within you the power to shift and adapt them so that they better meet your needs at various points in your life, trying to exist under the constraints of anything that doesn't fit will be a significant source of inner conflict (just like the 38D trying to breathe in a 32A). But when you understand that you are free to live by *your* rules—not those laid down by your partner or family of origin, where you work or where you worship—you also realize that you can rewrite them as needed. You can create a life that is tailor-made.

What are your present values, your north stars? What would you like to guide your choices today? Grab a pen and jot some down. If nothing comes immediately to mind, it may help to look at a menu of options and tick the ones that feel most like you. Here are some that have resonated with me over the years:

★ Social justice
★ Achievement
★ Time
★ Vulnerability
★ Kindness
★ Adventure
★ Loyalty
★ Perseverance
★ Financial stability
★ Patience
★ Tradition
★ Security
★ Faith/spirituality
★ Collaboration
★ Cooperation
★ Courage
★ Generosity
★ Leadership

★ Truth
★ Optimism
★ Fairness
★ Compassion
★ Diversity
★ Wisdom
★ Harmony
★ Humility
★ Fun
★ Responsibility
★ Independence
★ Learning
★ Service
★ Friendliness
★ Family
★ Humor
★ Respect
★ Reliability

Priorities and Habits

If values light the path you want to travel, then priorities are how you keep your foot on the gas. A priority, by definition, is one thing that is more important than another. And your priorities are how you embody those values through the way you spend your life's most precious currencies—everything from money and time to energy and emotional capacity to creativity and talent.

To prioritize a value is to do the work it requires. If you value cleanliness, then you will prioritize scrubbing the bathtub. If you value family time, then you'll prioritize an activity together. If you value mental wellness, you will prioritize quality sleep and space for quiet and regular therapy. If you value a healthy body, then you'll prioritize preparing nutritious foods. (I prioritize ice cream, for whatever that's worth.) As a woman in recovery, I can *value* sobriety all I want, but unless I'm doing the work of going to meetings, examining my triggers and resentments, practicing truth-telling and keeping clean my side of the street, then I'm only *talking* about sobriety—not prioritizing it.

Priorities are what take precedence. They get attention and resources before competing alternatives. And there are a lot of options competing, yes? Family, work, health, home, friends—you name it, everybody wants a piece of you.

The writer Kristi Coulter put it best in her book *Nothing Good Can Come from This*: "Do you remember the Enjoli perfume commercial from the 1970s? The chick who could bring home the bacon, fry it up in a pan, and never let you forget you're a man? I blame that bitch for a lot. For spreading the notion that women should have a career, keep house, and fuck their husbands, when the only sane thing to do is pick two and outsource the third."[4] So you've got to pick and choose, because if you try to prioritize *everything*, you will run out of time and energy and accomplish absolutely *nothing*.

Let's take a moment to consider your priorities.

As you look at the list below, undoubtedly you'll see some that resonate with you now, some that probably hit home in the past, some that will be most relevant in the future. The point is, if you're growing, your priorities will change over time, because *you* change over time. What you wanted as a kid in high school probably isn't the same thing you wanted after becoming a parent, if you are one. Your priorities should shift naturally over time; that's the very definition of personal evolution. The trick is to make sure your priorities are current.

★ Work/career
★ Saving money
★ Healing trauma
★ Organizing your home
★ Nutrition
★ Paying bills on time
★ Caring for children
★ Caring for parents
★ Self-care
★ Dealing with grief
★ Starting a business

★ Practicing faith
★ Personal growth
★ Taking a class
★ Marriage/intimacy
★ Medical needs
★ Travel/adventure
★ Making memories
★ Spirituality
★ Going to therapy
★ Having fun
★ Cleaning house
★ Recovery

- ★ Quality family time
- ★ Appearance
- ★ Earning money
- ★ Community involvement
- ★ Exercise
- ★ Paying off debt

If the most telling reflection of your values is your priorities, then the most telling reflection of your priorities is your habits. "Every action you take is a vote for the type of person you wish to become," wrote James Clear in *Atomic Habits*. "The most practical way to change *who* you are is to change *what* you do."[5] And, from Annie Dillard: "How we spend our days is, of course, how we spend our lives."[6]

Pop quiz: Are you doling out the currency of your life—the money in your pocket, the time in your day, your emotional and creative energy—in ways that reflect your current values? If not, where are the gaps? Who or what is getting the best parts of you? Is that what you intend?

Once you do the important work of clarifying your values (what you stand for) and your current priorities (those things that are more important than other things), it becomes easier to see how small actions on repeat can bring your vision into sharper view.

This is a powerful reckoning because it shows, pretty clearly, just where you are veering off the road . . . and how you can get back on.

But if you don't focus your headlights on your values and priorities now, there's a good chance you'll stay headed in the wrong direction as you move forward.

Measuring Success

There is an old adage in the business world that "you can't manage what you don't measure." But there are other metrics beyond the traditional appraisals of wealth, job titles, and accomplishments to evaluate how you're doing that may be more closely aligned with your values of today.

I first started thinking about alternative measurements back in 2010 when I read an article in the *Harvard Business Review*: "How Will You Measure Your Life?" by Clayton Christensen.[7] (That article later became a book by the same name.) I was on a plane headed to the East Coast and thought I'd thumb through the piece casually. It was so powerful that I had the whole thing marked up and highlighted in no time and, because I was so moved, I shared it with the woman seated across the aisle from me. She was a total stranger—but also a working mom, so really no stranger at all—and we talked about it the entire way to New York.

I scribbled on a yellow legal pad a list of questions—questions for which I didn't yet have answers and, in some cases, wouldn't have for years—but they spilled out, and it was my duty to capture them.

- What is the purpose of my life?
- What is the metric by which I'll measure success?
- What do I want my family's culture to be?
- What qualities do I admire and want to instill in my children?
- What do I want out of my marriage?

- What do I want out of my career?
- What can the people in my life reasonably expect from me? What do I "owe" them?
- My husband? Parents? Friends? Coworkers? Clients? Children? Myself?
- What can I contribute? To my family? To society? To my job?
- What do I want my legacy to be?
- How do I want to be known/remembered?
- What do I stand for?
- How do I prioritize my stakeholders?
- What am I afraid of?
- If money were no object, what would my profession be?
- If I were to go back to school, what would I study?
- In what ways do I disappoint myself? Others?
- What can I do better?
- What is my greatest treasure?

In his stunning poem "Sometimes," David Whyte writes about the power of questions that lead us to truth:

. . . *questions*
that can make
or unmake
a life,
questions
that have patiently
waited for you,
questions

that have no right
to go away.[8]

Questions that have no right to go away.

Sometimes the mere presence of big questions can feel like suffocating under a daunting weight, like being trapped under the nylon canopy of a hot-air balloon before it lifts off from the ground. But I think of the questions as the very air that makes flight possible. And the bigger the questions, the higher you can fly.

Perhaps I am so comfortable with questions because I was born with the nature to ask them; perhaps it's what journalism school trained me to do. Or, perhaps it's the belief that questions aren't the only things that have no right to go away; truth has no right to go away, either, and you cannot arrive at truth without inquiry and excavation.

The process of cross-examining your values, priorities, and alignment with each can be disruptive, yes—but how else do you get a question answered other than to ask it? Only you have the information these inquiries seek and, trust me, they're not going away until your answers—unfeigned and faithful to your deepest being—are considered.

Once you define success based on your own unique set of north stars, your life shifts drastically. You can begin to live with consistency, authenticity, and integrity, and you become freer than ever before to craft a dream and make it reality.

Unless, perhaps, the voice of Fear is telling you a different story?

Closing Exercise: *Measuring Success*

The traditional metrics of success—such as occupation, title, the size of your house or type of car you drive or the number of dollars in the bank—reflect just one, narrow aspect of life: professional/financial success. How can you assess other, less tangible aspects, such as the love you give and receive, your emotional health, your impact on others, the level of freedom you cultivate? What are the nontraditional ways you can measure progress against your unique set of values and priorities?

Second, and while this might at first feel like an assignment too morbid to even entertain, have you ever written out an obituary you'd be proud to see after you're gone? Surprisingly, this almost always turns out to be one of the most valuable exercises in my workshops because, by forcing you to think beyond this lifetime, you are able to evaluate what matters most from a perspective much different than where you're standing now. Don't be afraid to "go there."

4

How Fear Holds You Back

When our attitude toward fear becomes more welcoming and inquisitive, a fundamental shift occurs. Instead of spending our lives tensing up, we learn that we can connect with the freshness of the moment and relax.
—**Pema Chödrön**

Many years ago, I was talking with a friend who was at a relationship crossroads. (Actually, it was more of a T-intersection; the proverbial road she had been traveling was ending, and she had two choices: left or right.) She found herself stuck at the stop sign, so overwhelmed that she was paralyzed. She was absolutely consumed by the what-ifs associated with moving in either direction—worried what people might think of her if she turned one way and questioning her capacity to make it if she went the other.

The issue was not that she didn't *have* options, it was that she was too afraid to pick one.

I reminded my friend that fear is related to how we perceive ourselves in a given situation, and together we dug into the issue. For each concern she raised, I asked gently: What do you feel underneath that? Then, what's underneath *that*? We did this for close to a half hour. Layer by layer, bit by bit, we excavated the deeper truth: she was afraid of being alone.

My friend wasn't entirely comforted by this revelation—she thought it made her weak and stripped her of any sense of self-sufficiency—but it gave her something tangible to work on. With the help of her therapist, she remembered that the desire for connection and belonging is a basic human need and began to untangle the knot of self-judgment.

Some fear is natural, healthy, and essential for our survival as a species. For example, if a ferocious saltwater crocodile's strong jaws are about to chomp down on your leg, you *want* the brain to initiate the instantaneous cascade of signals that will shoot adrenaline into the body, draw oxygen-rich breath into the lungs, pump blood into the powerful muscles of the thighs, and make you RUN AWAY RIGHT NOW. In that way, the fear sparked by your innate survival instinct, the same instinct that helped our caveman ancestors survive and evolve, is inarguably your friend.

But when our reptilian brains apply those same impulses to less dangerous situations? Overkill.

For many of us, the fear response to what's listed above can feel, in the brain

> It's those outsized, primordial reactions to less fatal, even run-of-the-mill threats that often keep us stuck.

and the body, as intense as an impending chomp of the crocodile jaw, but it's those outsized, primordial reactions to less fatal, even run-of-the-mill threats that often keep us stuck.

Here are the most common fears revealed in responses from the survey I conducted in 2015 and refreshed in 2021:

- Concern over finances (specifically, not having sufficient money and resources to support the choices we want to make)
- Fear of failure (aka, sticking your neck out, only to have it broken)
- Fear of starting over (oh no, not again; been there, done that)
- Fear of criticism and ridicule (I'll be found out for who I really am, and proven as not good enough/smart enough/"enough" enough)
- Fear of change and the unknown (aka, sticking with the devil you know)

Of course, these only scratch the surface. The realm of possible concoctions of fears is limited only by experience and imagination; each of the eight billion souls alive now possesses its own unique mix based on physical, psychological, environmental, and familial experiences and circumstances.

Most of us know that unprocessed, dishonored fear can be a limiting factor in our lives, but I believe we underestimate just how powerful and destabilizing a force it is. The most important thing I know about fear is this: Fear that we do not honor is insidious—a crooked, guileful snake in the grass. Fear fights dirty.

It senses weak spots and preys on uncertainty. It makes us quit before we even begin.

> Fear fights dirty. It senses weak spots and preys on uncertainty. It makes us quit before we even begin.

At the same time, fear is one of the most authentic responses we have, holding so much raw truth even if, on its face, it appears to be a lie. You just have to be willing to admit the presence of your fear rather than deny it for the sake of a brave face. See it, feel it, hear what it is trying to tell you, and take the time to understand why. That is the first step in working *with* your fear rather than struggling *against* it.

Recognizing Fear

The dictionary defines fear as "a distressing emotion aroused by impending danger, evil or pain, whether the threat is real or imagined." I would add that fear is reflective of how a person perceives herself in a given situation, and it drives actions, reactions, and nonactions, too.

For example, if you perceive yourself as not very smart, you may hesitate to take on tasks that require you to publicly process or calculate or draw conclusions, perhaps because you're afraid you won't perform well and people will think less highly of you. If, on the other hand, you are confident in your cognitive thinking skills, you will be more confident in the reasonings and conclusions drawn from them.

If you fear yourself to be weak, or at least weaker than someone on the other end of a confrontation, then you may shy away from speaking your heart or participating in difficult conversations. But if you perceive yourself as articulate and strong, you may be more willing to share your thoughts and defend your point of view.

If you think your worth is dependent on your actions and accomplishments, but believe you fall short of the bar (whether that bar was set by yourself or by others) and then judge yourself negatively for that, you may find yourself trapped in the empty-but-endless, fear-based quest for perfection.

In order to protect ourselves from what we fear, we say "I can't." It's classic risk management, a trusty defense mechanism that prevents us from getting physically hurt, emotionally disappointed, embarrassed or judged or vulnerable—all feelings we don't want to feel. But it also keeps us peeking out from behind the window shades when we are meant to be out exploring the world. That's a shame, because we won't ever feel the joy of grass between our toes if we're too scared to kick off our boots.

Think of the range of scenarios where "I can't" might be the first reaction, before you've even had the chance to adequately consider whether you, in fact, can.

- A compelling position opens up at work: "I can't leave where I am."
- You need to have a long-overdue, courageous conversation with a family member: "Yeah, right. That would be a freakin' disaster."
- A friend extends an invitation to do something unfamiliar and unexpected: "That's ridiculous. No way."

- A new love interest appears, though maybe a little too soon after your heart has been broken to bits: "Nope. I can't put myself out there again."
- Someone proposes you search for a job different from the one that is making you miserable: "That's just not possible."
- You want to go back to school: "My family would never go for it."
- Someone suggests you go to therapy to work with past trauma: "Absolutely not. I can't touch that."
- You're faced with the decision to leave an unhappy relationship: "I'm not strong enough."

Let's pick apart one of these: the idea of going back to school in order to learn a new skill or subject matter, or to go deeper on experience or expertise you already have.

This could require dropping out of the workforce to create time and energy; it could mean pulling back partially; or you could be challenged to add it to your existing plate. When a person feels stuck, it's easy to point a finger at an external force as the reason why she shouldn't pursue such a thing (hence, "My family would never go for that."). But, if she were able to be more honest about the fears associated with the idea, the more accurate hesitation might sound more like this:

- "I am afraid that I am too old to start over and I've missed my chance."
- "I'm anxious I won't be able to find a job making more money and the investment of time, money, and energy will be wasted."

- "I fear that my family won't support me or pick up the slack while I focus on this, and I'm already exhausted as it is. I'm afraid I can't do it all."
- "I don't think I'm smart enough."

Any statement that begins with "I worry . . ." or "I'm concerned . . ." or "I suspect . . ." typically is followed up with the articulation of some kind of fear, even if it masquerades as concern about other people. For example, "I fear my family won't support me," might be code for "I worry that *my family doesn't love me enough* to support me." This comes back to how a person perceives herself in a situation.

The Pipsqueak Twerp

Each of us has a voice in our head. The term in psychology is "inner speech." Eckhart Tolle calls it "the voice of the ego." Steven Pressfield, who wrote *The War of Art*, calls it "the voice of resistance." Michael Singer, author of *The Untethered Soul*, calls his voice(s) "the roommates who never shut up." (That last one feels like a spot-on assessment to me; in fact, Ethan Kross, who wrote the book *Chatter: The Voice in Our Head, Why It Matters, and How to Harness It*, estimates that your inner voice talks at the rate of 320 State of the Union addresses each day: "The voice in your head is a very fast talker."[1])

Whatever name we know it by, that inner voice is, by most accounts, a real pain in the rump. It never says *nice* things.

Omigosh, you're so smart! Your hair looks amazing today! You're really doing a terrific job at life! No, it's actually quite the downer.

That's because this unrelenting voice in your head is the voice of fear. It is the play-by-play announcer of every negative observation and judgment, the source of all shitty self-talk. It will say all kinds of nasty, limiting, untrue things to you and therefore is not to be trusted. (This is different than the voice of your soul, which we'll talk about in the next chapter.)

I call my nasty inner voice "the Pipsqueak Twerp" and, I have no qualms in telling you, he can be a real motherfucker. (He's not necessarily *trying* to be that way; he's just scared and doesn't know any better.)

On a regular day, I can look at my journey thus far and honor it:

Wow, baby, look at how far you've come! You put the pin in your family's long history of untreated alcoholism. You didn't look away when depression threatened to undo you; instead, you see the doctors and do the things they prescribe, including taking the medicine you were afraid to take. You had the cajones to fly without a net to quit a work environment that wasn't working for you and, in its place, create something entirely new. You healed your heart so that you could love again. You're brave and unique and you have learned so much the hard way. God, I love you! Keep on doing what you're doing.

On a bad day, however, the Pipsqueak Twerp sings a grossly different tune. (Think John Wayne here.)

Why, you're nothin' but a sad, lily-livered, pill-poppin' drunk. Your expectations are sky-high and you're way too quick to criticize—no wonder your husband didn't want to be married to you anymore! No doubt you'll ruin the second the same way you ruined the first. And your poor kids; there's no telling the countless ways you're going to fuck them up. When they end up on the therapist's couch, it will be entirely because of you. Who are you to be giving advice to anyone. You're a pathetic Piece of Shit.

I shared that once during a workshop and the room fell ghostly silent. I watched tears fall from the eyes glued on me. Participants were heartbroken that a person—especially one they liked and respected, and who was ostensibly teaching about how to curtail such things—could speak to themselves so mercilessly. "I remember thinking, what the F?!," one woman wrote to me later. "This wise, gorgeous, put-together woman says THAT to herself?! How cruel and woefully untrue. It was really groundbreaking for me to have you put words to that inner critic and know even YOU, our brave teacher, could ever think that."

When I asked students to put pen to paper and capture some of the horrible things their inner voices said to *them,* they quickly realized the very same kind of attacks were happening within their psyches; they were only shocked because they hadn't heard the words spoken aloud before. Some hard-to-stomach verbatims, all shared here with permission:

"You're nuthin'. You don't fit anywhere, you have no direction, no aspiration, and you're a sad excuse for an adult."

"You're fat, ugly, and fucked up."

"You will never be loved in a way you believe is true."

"You're so fucking stupid! What are you THINKING?"

"I don't know how you thought you could pull this off but you can't—and you have no fucking right to even try."

"You're worthless. You were ruined out of the gate."

"No wonder you're single and alone. No one will ever love a broken, fractured mess of a human like you."

"You can't start your own business, you don't know shit about starting a business. Why would anyone want to hire you? Get a fucking grip."

"Why did you just say that? No one cares what you think. Stop talking, you freaking idiot."

One woman volunteered during a retreat that the voice in her head sounded exactly like her mother's: "You're a Perpetual Disappointment!" she screamed, and fifty hearts broke simultaneously. My own heart is still piecing itself back together after that.

The good news is that there are things you can do to take away or at least turn down the volume on that voice and reduce its power. (At first you'll learn how to turn down the volume; eventually you'll be able to change the channel.) One trick to neutralizing your Pipsqueak Twerp, which I picked up from my good friend Scott Stabile, is to turn the voice into a character—a caricature or a villain, perhaps—that you won't take very seriously. It can help to give your voice a name (Scott called his "Gloria"), a distinctly awful look and sound, even a signature word or phrase. The more ghastly the persona, the more easily you'll identify it when it starts mouthing off and the more quickly it will diminish its own credibility.

Then, don't let that voice talk down to you or allow untrue statements to go unchallenged. Stand up for yourself! Talk back in truth! I've had many a conversation this way—sometimes entirely within my own head, sometimes out loud—and it never fails to provide the perspective I need to feel less afraid of the situation at hand.

The Inner Thorn

In *The Untethered Soul,* Michael Singer devotes a chapter to the idea of "the inner thorn," a powerful concept I have used as a jumping-off point in my teaching for years. To make the abstract more tangible, Singer describes a person with a thorn embedded in his arm. Because the thorn touches a nerve and causes great pain, the person designs elaborate protective equipment and takes significant evasive maneuvers to keep the thorn from bumping up against anything that would disturb it. He can't sleep, can't get close to anyone, can't find comfort.

"The truth is, the thorn completely runs your entire life," Singer writes. "It affects all your decisions, including where you go, whom you're comfortable with, and who's comfortable with you. It determines where you're allowed to work, what house you can live in, and what kind of bed you can sleep on at night. When it's all said and done, that thorn is running every aspect of your life."[2]

Our fears are a lot like inner thorns. We build protections

that may have served us well at one time but now stand as a barrier to potential.

A woman I'll call Amy participated in two back-to-back sessions of one of my online courses. ("I'm hooked!" she joked.) Near the conclusion of the second six-week class, she wrote me about the part of her life she had identified as demanding change and, in doing so, revealed her inner thorn. "It is my drinking. Pure and simple. And it has been the eight-hundred-pound gorilla in the room for a long, long time. I have had short periods of sobriety over the years but have never been able to make it stick. I have read all the quit lit, all the blogs, all the Instagrams," she wrote. "For me, the drinking goes hand in hand with the loneliness that I struggle with. My loneliness is bone-marrow deep. It is always there. Even in a crowd. And I drink to numb it, make it go away. I have never married nor had children, which is the source of tremendous sadness. The feeling of being not good enough, not pretty enough, not chosen. It's all so difficult to feel."

I wrote back: "Being able to name this thing is a turning point. To see it clearly, to know what it is you're working with, is a gift because it shows you the way forward. Now is the time to dig in more to the loneliness. Embrace it, get intimate with what it is really telling you, but don't be afraid of it. Don't look away, because this is where your healing is."

Fear as a Compass to Truth

Feeling tough feelings—the ones that make you weep in powerlessness or shame, burn in white-hot rage, recoil in self-loathing and disgust—can seem more than merely uncomfortable, especially if your system is rooted in trauma. It can feel literally unbearable, like you might prefer to claw off your own skin.

But when you use fear to signal an entry point, you can follow the thread and get closer to the real issue. That is one reason fear isn't something in itself to be feared; in fact, fear can be quite an asset when handled with curiosity rather than consternation, compassion instead of contempt. And, ultimately, feeling it heals it.

Here are a few responses from the survey that show just how avoidant we can be to fear and the emotions we humans are terrified to experience.

- "I don't want to go through the pain."
- "Sometimes I just want to run away from all my problems but I know that's not the solution."
- "I seem to have wired myself to become anxious about change, so I avoid the subject entirely . . . and stay stuck."
- "My fear is taking over my chances."

As an alternative to simply falling into step with your fear, try to listen for the clues in the language you use when responding to something that sparks it. Do you hear an "I can't"? An "I'm not _____ enough"? Observe your gut reactions and you may find the same responses repeated often, reflexively. Then, to move beyond the typical response of "I can't," you can embrace the discipline to peer deep beneath the surface to see what is really triggering your fears.

Working with fear is like picking up a big rock only to find all the creepy crawlies that live in the dirt beneath. The instinct is to drop the rock and run—but that does nothing to address what underlies your fear, it just means you've chosen not to look at it. Problems are not solved by avoidance. You've got to engage those creepy crawlies in the eye, no matter how nasty they are.

Start in the Body

In the group gatherings I lead, we spend a good chunk of time working with fear: where it is driving the agenda, how it makes us feel, what it makes us do in response. We may start in the head but then move into the body. My typical workshop is a combination of yoga *asana* (physical postures done on the mat) and deep emotional self-exploration. We move and breathe and write and connect. We ask ourselves tough questions and peel back the BS to get to the honest answers. We laugh and we cry. It's basically three hours of soul-baring and fear-busting and action planning, all set in the safe space of a yoga studio.

Robyn came to one of my New Year's retreats at the Kripalu Center for Yoga & Health in Massachusetts. As a longtime psychotherapist and certified sex coach who teaches people about love and intimacy and the ancient art of tantra, Robyn knows a lot about bodies and she is very in tune with her own.

The irony of her story was that she didn't feel particularly stuck going into the long weekend—she was there because the friend she was with had chosen the workshop topic—but, come to think of it, there *was* this nagging pain in her hip . . . *and* her back . . . oh, and she *had* been working with a coach to lose some unwanted weight and improve her overall health.

In the first evening's yoga practice, I guided the group to their backs for a series of simple, repetitive movements designed to awaken the body bit by bit: easy pelvic tilts forward and back, slow-motion windshield wipers for the hip flexors and glutes, gentle twists to explore the spine and hips. You'll hear it said often in the yoga community that grief, fear, trauma, and other kinds of negative energy get "stored" specifically in the hips, and there is some debate whether that's a scientific fact—but for many, including me, there is no argument: the proof is in the practice.

That was certainly Robyn's experience that weekend. As she moved her body, she also moved long-locked-away grief from when her mother had passed away when Robyn was just ten. "Holy shit," Robyn told me later. "I found grief in my clenched muscles, my painful joints, in tight places in my body that hurt when I moved in ways that used to be easy. I touched stuff that was *so deep*."

The big realization, she said, was understanding the connection between her present and her past: "I'm carrying grief and I'm carrying weight and they're one and the same." She was also carrying a fear of feeling her feelings. With that sudden clarity, Robyn could see the decades of sadness and despair she had been holding, as well as the patterns and habits around food she had cultivated over the years to hide or distract from that grief. *She had been terrified of actually feeling her pain.*

So, right then and there, she let the emotions come, up and out and in full force. She wept off and on—both in grief and relief of releasing the fear of experiencing it—for the rest of the weekend. And as she put together the playbook that would guide her next action steps, Robyn committed to amping up her self-love practice. And that's exactly what she did: on the other side of the retreat, she returned to yoga practice, moved her body every day, and traded the food plan she had been working on with her health coach for a more intuitive approach. The result? When most of us gained twenty pounds during the first year of COVID-19 lockdown, Robyn lost twenty—and, within the next year, her cholesterol levels were down and other cardiovascular markers had either normalized or improved.

Robyn credits the safe energy of the workshop's environment and the gentle, compassionate pace of the yoga practice for allowing her body to identify the fear of actually feeling the grief she had bottled up after her mother's death. Once the body was heard, Robyn said she was able to commit to her healing with radical self-honesty, consistency, accountability, and, most of all, love.

"I've had revealing experiences before in other places and I would make a commitment but then I wouldn't follow through, or I'd follow through just a little bit and then it would drop off," she told me eighteen months after the experience. "The difference this time is that I didn't close up after those three days, and what I worked on that weekend has really actualized in my life.

"The step-by-step structure of the workshop and the provocative questions guided me and allowed me to work through something very specific. I had these huge aha moments about what I needed actually to work toward and shift in my life, and it really stuck. It was very, very powerful. I really did what I set out to do."

As Robyn's story shows, people often believe they are stuck in one particular area—but, with some digging, discover the true problem they are grappling with is a symptom of something that is seated much deeper, or perhaps is a doorway to an issue altogether different. Each situation or concern comes with its own bucket of fears.

Fear, Values, and Other People's Judgments

Just as values shape our desires, they shape our fears, too. That's because, in many ways, they are directly connected.

In the initial survey I conducted, so many respondents shared fears about change that pointed back to their status as a parent or a child: "I'm waiting for my children to grow." "I'm afraid my reasons to leave aren't good enough to rip apart my family." "I need to be here for my children rather than chasing dreams." "I don't want to ruin my kids' lives." "I cannot move anywhere until my parents pass on." "I have lots of dreams, but feel I would be letting my family down if I try to pursue them as their needs come first and I would be neglectful in my duties as a mother."

What bubbles to the surface in these comments is the value of family, yes—but that's not all. Imbedded there, too, is society's judgment that parents should be selfless, and that a parent who places her needs at the top of the priority list is anything but.

Comments also highlighted fears of being perceived by others as lacking values. "Am I being greedy? Shouldn't I be grateful for what I already have?" "It is my ego that's afraid of change." "It sounds selfish, I know . . . but I need to start helping myself before I drown." So, the fear isn't just the potentiality of ruining a child's life, but about being perceived or labeled as the kind of parent who would *willfully* do it.

In Chapter 2, we discussed how the opinions and expectations of Other People—who are all too eager to dispense them, aren't they, sonsofbitches bless their hearts—can spark within us the "indigestion of shoulds."

The indigestion typically rises up from two different but related worries. First, there is what someone could *think* or *say* about you in reaction to a choice you make, whether the topic is changing jobs or shifting the dynamics of a relationship or undertaking sobriety—anything that threatens the status quo, really. What makes this fear so powerful is that you fear those judgments just might mirror what the Pipsqueak Twerp has to say if you were to do the thing or say the thing or change the thing that is keeping you stuck.

The second is what they might actually *do* in response.

Fill in the blank for the fears that resonate most strongly with you. "If I do/say/change something, they will _____:"

- think poorly of me
- think I'm weak
- think I'm selfish
- take it personally and make it about them
- question my abilities
- question my sanity
- lose faith in me
- lose respect for me

- not want to be around me
- badmouth me to others
- punish me somehow

All of this serves to keep us conforming to everybody else's expectations for our lives, being good little doobies, generally toeing the line—which, in many cases, keeps us stuck where we don't want to be. As Brené Brown so perfectly put it: "You can't ever do anything brave if you're wearing the straitjacket of 'What will people think?!'"[3]

Perhaps the more valuable question is less about what anyone else thinks of you, and more about what we think of ourselves. For example, if you do the thing that needs to be done/say the thing that needs to be said/change the thing that needs to be changed, will you think poorly of yourself? Think you're weak or selfish? Question your abilities or sanity or judgment? Lose respect for or faith in yourself? Punish yourself?

Or, might you actually think *more* of yourself? Feel more capable, more powerful? Stand tall on your values and discernment? Gain a deeper respect for the person you're becoming?

I have walked through the fires of Other People's disappointment and can report back from the front lines that it just doesn't burn the way I thought it would. I mean, it burns . . . but burns heal eventually. If you can trust me on that, perhaps you can make a promise to no longer shush the screaming of your gut, to not hide the truth of what you know, not from yourself and not from anyone else, to not stifle the voice that demands to speak, even if you are the only one who hears it at first.

Promise you will not abandon yourself, ever again, by placing someone else's opinion of you above your own.

Promise you won't live this life in a straitjacket simply because you're afraid.

Promise you will not abandon yourself, ever again, by placing someone else's opinion of you above your own.

It's Not About Being Fearless

I'm sure you've heard the saying "Feel the fear and do it anyway." That's catchy, for sure, but I think the mantra is missing a step because I do not know a single human—no matter how evolved—who is truly fearless or devoid of any worry. And yet, the deepest part within us—our soul—is indeed free of fear. What a lovely paradox.

Fear cannot be eradicated from our human experience. So, how do you move from a place of fear to a place of trust? First, by accepting that it probably isn't going anywhere and instead learning to use it in a constructive manner. The question is: How?

Pema Chödrön smiles at her fear. Anne Lamott befriends it. Elizabeth Gilbert tells hers that it can sit in the car but it cannot drive. What these approaches have in common is the recognition that none of us is completely fearless, and fear will be a life-long companion, so best to find a way to move forward together.

We will talk in Chapter 7 about how to gently move fear to

the side and instead strategically evaluate trade-offs and consequences for a given situation. For now, though, just putting hesitation into the context of fear is an excellent start for learning how to work with it, instead of feeling overwhelmed or immobilized by it. Because that is where you begin to find the truth.

> If you say you're stuck, I won't believe you. But if you say you feel scared—or that you're afraid to feel something potentially scary such as loneliness, powerlessness, fury, grief, even something as terrifying as being truly seen—I will hold you.

Final thought: If you say you're stuck, I won't believe you. But if you say you feel scared—or that you're afraid to feel something potentially scary such as loneliness, powerlessness, fury, grief, even something as terrifying as being truly seen—I will hold you. So please don't default to "I can't." Instead, say what is more true:

"I'm afraid I can't learn how to do this."

"That feels too risky right now."

"I'm afraid of getting hurt."

Looking more objectively and forgivingly at your fear can keep your options open and potential limitless—which can, in turn, reshape your choices, your circumstances, your whole reality, really. And, over time, you will be able to step solidly into your most joyful truth: "I can."

The truth about fears is they may be universal *feelings,* but they aren't facts, and they most certainly are not permanent. And if you think you don't have it in you to put on your shit-kickers and take care of business, darling, I suggest you think again.

Closing Exercise: *Examining Your Fears*

Grab a pen and paper. Set a timer for three minutes and list as many of your fears as you possibly can. Don't judge them as irrational, or omit because you think you should be past that by now. Just go for three minutes. Now, imagine those fears as a pile of rocks. Pick up just three of the biggest ones for a more thorough examination. Turn them over in your hands, one by one, and check them from all sides. Notice the ground under the rock, especially the impression in the dirt and the creepy crawlies that remain. What's *really* underneath that fear? Keep challenging yourself to go deeper and deeper by asking at least four times: *What is it that I* really *fear here?*

When you come to an answer that you feel in your body—perhaps a quickening heart rate, a fleeting sense of dizziness, even the urge to rush to the bathroom—recognize the physical response to the emotions that arise. Then notice and, without judgment, try to identify the fear that underlies it all. Hold that fear gently, with compassion and curiosity, and let it guide you to new epiphanies and perspectives. Don't look away. Rather, see it and love it and let it be your compass, not the obstruction on your path.

Part II

Moving from Fear to Choice

5

Who Do You Think You Are?

We are waiting for permission, for examples. But what if you are the example?
—**Jedidiah Jenkins**

want to say, right out of the gate, that this is the chapter I am most excited for you to read. This is where it's going to get really deep and really good. Like, *gooooooood*. Because this is where we get to explore God.

Wait! Don't run! This won't be overly academic or dogmatic or woo-woo. (Well, okay, it's gonna be pretty woo-woo. But in the good way!) This is what I believe could be *the* difference maker when it comes to breaking free from whatever is holding you back right now.

A Fundamental Belief

I have been fascinated by the idea of "God" since I was small because it was always in the background of my Catholic up-bringing. Despite the best efforts of the nuns at St. Bernadette grade school and, later, Ursuline Academy ("Home for Way-ward Girls," I always add with a snicker), I just couldn't get with the program. All those rituals—the exhausting sit/stand/kneel loop of Mass—felt like some weird, automaton charade.

In high school, I full-on rebelled against it. I tried to wiggle out of going to religion class on, ahem, religious grounds. *Atheists don't go to religion class,* I asserted. *They do here,* was the response. There was just too much in the Church's teachings and operations that represented clear south stars to me, like megaton spotlights in space, blinking on and off, forbidding me to look away. *You don't like gay people? Divorce is a sin? Women can't be ordained? Pedophile priests repeatedly get swept under the rug? Fuck off, fuck off, fuck off.*

But what really tripped me up was the idea of God "out there" rather than "in here."

Perhaps that reveals a fundamental sense of self-centeredness, but my reaction to being separate from the Divine was somehow: *What am I, cat vomit?* Because when I looked around, I felt that sense of awesomeness in other beings: my friends, my pets, the trees, the stars. I felt it within me, too, even if the voices of authority weren't shy about reminding me of the size of my britches. The idea of being a "child of God" didn't resonate; I thought I was a child of my parents and that was it. To me, that power dynamic of "other" or "above" felt unnecessarily false, so I chose not to fake it. After my high school graduation ceremony, I never again went willingly to Mass, save the occasional family funeral or wedding. But I was still interested and investigating.

In college, I studied other major world religions beyond Christianity—not because I was "looking for God," per se, but because I had adopted a firm point of view (as teenagers have been known to do) that organized religion was nothing but an attempt at social control through fear, and I was curious if others elsewhere approached it in the same way. Surprisingly, as I learned about some of the Eastern philosophies, namely Buddhism and Hinduism, there was a tinge of resonance: concepts like reincarnation and karma didn't feel *entirely* wacky; Buddhism's Eightfold Path, with its practices like right speech, right action, and right mindfulness, seemed more intuitive, more sensible than the bellowing dogma of the Ten Commandments I was raised on.

But mostly, I was attracted to the idea that "God" could be something other than The Old Dude in The Sky, that it could be *energy*, that it could be everywhere, in all of us.

I kept pondering the subject—even, for a brief while, changing my college major from journalism to religious studies before changing it back—until I couldn't deny that I believed in *something*, I just couldn't put a name on it. It would be years later, when I came to the yoga mat, that I finally did.

What I believed in was my Self. "Self" with a capital S.

Spirit.

Soul.

Source.

Enter yoga, which, by definition, is the union of the body to the Self, the connection of the God within to the God around.

Yoga, my homecoming.

Yoga: More Than a Pose

I once heard it said that you don't have to have your shit together to go to yoga; you go to yoga to get your shit together.

I first gave it a try at age twenty-six, just a couple weeks after I initiated divorce from my first marriage (yeah, technically I was married once before "my first marriage," but I don't count that one because it lasted all of thirty seconds; I just took a mulligan and moved on). I was all sorts of things, but "having my shit together" was not even close to how I'd describe it.

I'm not sure what made me buy that Rodney Yee VHS tape. (Was it the allure of the ponytail? The serene mountain backdrop on the cover?) I stuck it in my VCR one night and thought, *Why the hell not?* I remember the deep clink of the Tibetan chimes. It was a brand-new sound, one that reverberated in my chest. That sound seemed to brush up against something within me that felt new and unfamiliar, yet ancient and omnipresent at the same time.

I couldn't touch my toes in the beginning, but the feeling of the breath moving in and out was satisfying in a different way, mesmerizing almost, as was the quiet I experienced when my mind was fixated on being right there, with myself, instead of anywhere and everywhere else. So, I stuck with it, following that one tape over and over again, until I committed it to memory, then I added another and memorized that one, too. Only then did I screw up the guts to try a class in a studio.

I was petrified on the way in, not knowing what to expect or how I'd "perform"—and positively flying on the way out.

There was something about breathing in unison with others

that made me feel more connected to my Self. I loved the gentle reminders, in the face of discomfort or distraction, to come back to the awareness of my body, to come back to the moment. I had no idea who that was yet but, my god, I loved the way the beautiful Russian girl leading the class—so strong, poised, and exuding a sense of real peace—seemed to embody it. I wanted what she had.

The pace of practice, so much slower than my otherwise frantic life, was a welcome departure—although that quiet time at the end of practice in *savasana* ("corpse pose") was the purest kind of torture. Every class, I had to fight the temptation to roll up my mat and sneak out before it began, as so many anxious folks do when they first come to the practice. Those few minutes lying flat on my back, eyes closed, with a brain that *could not shut up,* made each of my cells twitch and burn in agitated impatience. It just felt so *unnatural,* so grossly unproductive, to lay there and do nothing, mostly because my mind was accustomed either to regurgitating the past, stressing about the future, or checking out completely to avoid both.

I had no idea how to simply sit with my heartbeat and use that time to notice how I felt.

I didn't know how to breathe in a manner that invited that kind of presence and awareness.

I had no connection to the voice deep within me—the one who speaks in stillness—because I never slowed down enough or became quiet enough to hear her.

And because she didn't know how to do much more than whisper back then, because she wasn't as demanding as all the other voices who shouted lies they didn't yet know were lies, I didn't know to give her my attention.

But there was something about those days when I would rush out of the office after ten or twelve hours and speed toward the studio, swapping power heels for yoga pants somewhere between the fourth and fifth gears, and settle my amped-up body onto my mat, when I'd listen to my teacher Pam's soothing voice invite me to settle down and pay attention to the breath moving in and out of my lungs. She likened the thoughts passing rapid-fire through my consciousness to a film strip playing on a movie projector, and encouraged me to slow down the playback, even taking scissors to the film between frames in order to add more space between them. Only then did I begin to learn about the virtue and magnificence of being truly, wholly *there*. Present.

I began to understand one of the most fundamental teachings of yoga: we are, as Vonnegut put it, human *beings*, not human *doings*. This is how I learned to stop running away from my feelings. This is how I learned to stay. This is how I learned to return to my Self. And, eventually, those quiet moments in the dark, accompanied by the ocean waves of my breath, became a glorious and magical quiet, and my entire being craved more of it. Still does.

Within a few years, my passion reached the point that I was ready to learn to teach, so I enrolled in a training program even as my PR job churned on relentlessly—nine months of weekend immersions and evening classes and studying whenever I could fit it in. I had expected that immersion to teach me how to twist and shimmy my body into more advanced, pretzel-like shapes and balance on my head or my hands. *Party tricks!* But I got way more than I bargained for as the concepts raised during practice, such as acceptance and non-attachment and divinity within, seeped into my day-to-day consciousness, replacing my desire for material success with a desire for inner contentment. And when my teacher said, "Control the body and you can control the breath; control the breath and you can control the mind," I was forever hooked—because if there's one thing a type-A, Enneagram-8 alcoholic appreciates, it's control.

What would surprise me most was understanding that the way to gain control is to relinquish it.

The way to gain control is to *relinquish* it.

Monkey Mind and The Eight Limbs

(How's *that* for a band name?)

Looking back, it is easy to understand that sense of resonance I felt back in college when first introduced to the tenets of Buddhism and Hinduism (save its abhorrent caste system). They both originated in ancient India, the same birthplace as yoga, with Buddhism growing out of Hinduism. Yoga is actually one of the six schools of Hindu philosophy.

One of yoga's most sacred texts—*The Yoga Sutras of Patanjali*, the sage after which the writings are named—introduces the practice this way: "Yoga is the cessation of the fluctuations of the mind."[1] Fluctuations, modifications, gyrations, whirlings, ridiculous fucking mental gymnastics—whatever you call it, it's about trying to quiet down that bouncing, chattering, howling brain we often call "monkey mind" (insert gif of crazy monkey in a cage, jumping to and fro, unable to settle down).

Sometimes the mind's chatter is the nasty stuff of the Pip-squeak Twerp (or whatever you call your inner critic); sometimes it is truly, no pun intended, just a string of mindless thoughts: *My god, the skin on my heel is so rough! Who's sexier: old Sam Elliott or young Paul Newman? Wonder what gross concoction the pumpkin spice maniacs are gonna push this year . . . Pop-Tarts? Hard seltzer? Condoms? Ugh, I'm so bloated. Ooh! I should order that book before I forget. (Types a-m-a-z-o . . .)* The chatter, whether good, bad, or indifferent, just doesn't want to stop.

What yoga teaches is to slow those thoughts down—not so you can catch them and engage with them, but so you can create some space between them, which allows you to be more conscious in choosing *not* to engage with them. It's like putting a collar and leash on the monkey so you can gently pull his attention back toward you as part of an effort to calm him down. You teach the monkey there is nothing he needs to escape from by cultivating an environment that's quieter, more peaceful, less demanding of an escape route. And, eventually, you get to show the monkey the bliss of connecting to the center of universal consciousness, "the Source."

That, right there, is pretty much the essence of what Patanjali called "the eight limbs of yoga." They map out a progression that funnels our attention inward, beginning with society at large, then to the body, then the mind, and, finally, the spirit. We don't start with bliss; we work our way there. One element flows into the next, in sequence.

Here's a brief overview:

The first two limbs—*yamas* and *niyamas*—are essentially ethical guidelines. They cover how one should interact with the world around him (don't kill, don't lie, don't steal, etc.) and also manage oneself (keep clean, have discipline, reflect on the spiritual, surrender to a higher power, etc.).

The next limb—*asana*—refers in its purest form to holding a steady, comfortable seat that would be suitable for meditation . . . but if you've ever tried to sit cross-legged and still for any length of time, you'll know that requires a few things of the body: open hips, a tall spine supported by strong core muscles, and the ability to stay present in spite of some discomfort. Practicing *asana,* the physical poses of yoga, helps open the body where it needs to be open and strengthens it where it needs to be stable, all to facilitate untroubled sitting so you can get to the *really* good part.

The fourth limb of yoga—*pranayama*—refers to breathing techniques that help master the flow of *prana,* or "life force." They can have varying effects on the body (some practices are calming, others energizing, some emphasize flowing, some chop the breath up into pieces or restrain it for a period) but one underlying purpose is to give the mind something on which to focus in order to stay grounded in the present moment.

Limbs five, six, and seven—*pratyahara, dharana,* and *dhyana*—refer, respectively, to drawing the physical senses (such as smell or sight or hearing) away from the external environment and inward instead; focusing the mind's concentration, often on the breath, a word, or an object like a candle; and, eventually, being absorbed into the state of meditation.

The last limb—*samadhi*—refers to the enlightenment, or "bliss," that comes with being one with the divine. (*Samadhi* is also the ultimate destination on Buddhism's Noble Eightfold Path.)

There are thousands of books, journal articles, and blog posts that can offer more detail and context about the eight limbs, though that level of detail isn't necessary for our purpose here. I do, however, want to go a little deeper on three aspects related to the limbs—the power of movement, breath, and mindfulness/meditation—to add to the incredible wisdom of the ancients what modern science has taught us.

Movement as Medicine

Practicing yoga *asana*—the physical postures—which can be done standing, seated, or lying down, does more than help improve strength, balance, and flexibility. Asana can help generate both mobility and stability in major joints like shoulders and hips; strengthen lower back and pelvic floor muscles; counter the effects of being hunched over computers and devices by opening the chest wall and keeping the spine more erect; reduce inflammation and pain; promote digestion and elimination; improve lung capacity and reduce blood pressure; support better sleep, reduce injury; improve proprioception (the sense of the body and its movements in the space around it) and overall awareness of what's going on in the body and the function of its systems.

In addition, yoga is often a recommended part of the treatment plan for anxiety, depression, and post-traumatic stress disorder (PTSD). Psychiatrist Bessel van der Kolk, author of *The Body Keeps the Score* and a leading expert in how trauma affects the brain and body, regularly points to yoga as a way to help heal trauma. As he explained at Kripalu:

"When people think about trauma, they generally think of it as a historical event that happened some time ago. Trauma is actually the residue from the past as it settles into your body. It's located inside your own skin. When people are traumatized, they become afraid of their physical sensations; their breathing becomes shallow, and they become uptight and frightened about what they're feeling inside. When you slow down your breathing with yoga, you can increase your heart rate variability, and that decreases stress. Yoga opens you up to feeling every aspect of your body's sensations. It's a gentle, safe way for people to befriend their bodies, where the trauma of the past is stored."[2]

Impact of Breath on the Nervous System

The scientific reason yoga works so well to help address things like depression, anxiety, and healing trauma lies in the connection between the breath and the body's nervous system, which has two parts: the sympathetic nervous system, the one that sparks your fight, flight, or freeze response, and the parasympathetic nervous system, which promotes relaxation and calm when stimulated.

The sympathetic nervous system (SNS) is the one that regulates the body's sensitivity for danger. When activated, the brain signals the adrenal glands to dump cortisol and adrenaline into the blood stream, presses pause on the digestive system, and redirects all that hormone-rich blood to the heart, lungs, and big muscles like your thighs. This stress response is terrific if you're about to be run over by an oncoming train and need to hop off the tracks quickly, but it's pure overkill when the situation involves arguing with your partner or hearing criticism from your boss.

It is the job of the parasympathetic nervous system (PNS) to bring things down. When the PNS is activated, the cells in the brain and the gut start releasing serotonin, which promotes relaxation, and the pituitary gland, located in the brain roughly behind the "third eye," lets loose with some oxytocin (often called "the love hormone"). All of that has the effect of lowering blood pressure and heart rate, slowing breath, aiding digestion, and generally feeling more chill. That's why the activation of the parasympathetic nervous system is often dubbed "rest and digest" in contrast to "fight or flight." It unwinds your stress.

See for yourself. Pause here and breathe more deeply. You may notice that simply shifting your attention to the breath will make your inhale naturally lengthen, and you'll exhale a little more fully. Maybe wiggle your jaw around a little to let go of some tension you may not even realize has been hiding there. Perhaps your shoulders can relax, falling down from your ears. (I have a girlfriend who responds particularly well to the cue: "Drop your shoulder earrings.")

Now notice: Are you breathing through your nose or mouth? If it's the latter, don't stress, but see about shifting those inhales and exhales to come in and out of your nose. As my teacher taught me: the mouth is for eating, the nose is for breathing. That's because breathing through the nose filters dust and germs from the air as it enters the nostrils. The nose then heats and moistens that air for easier absorption of oxygen. Breathing through the mouth, on the other hand, dries out the air, among other unhelpful things. That's not to say you *can't* breathe this way (it takes just one snotty nose to be extra grateful for the ability to breathe through the mouth!), but it isn't *optimal*. Keep breathing.

What's happening inside your body as you breathe is simple, yet profound. The act of breathing is an exchange of air between the atmosphere and your lungs. It can be automatic, forced, or controlled. The diaphragm, that dome-shaped muscle that rests beneath the lungs, is the key. It works like a pump: on the inhale, the diaphragm contracts, drawing down toward the belly, and brings air into the lungs; on the exhale, the diaphragm relaxes and returns to its dome shape, moving back toward the lungs and forcing the air out.

Feel a little more relaxed already? That's your breath activating the parasympathetic nervous system.

Your respiratory rhythm directly and indirectly affects the entire body system and, with deep breathing, you stimulate the vagus nerve. That's the long connection between the brain and the gut that influences things like your mood, anxiety, heart rate, digestion, and immune response. Your body calms down and you can finally hear your deeper Self.

"Your breath listens wholeheartedly to all that it meets, staying with you no matter what arises. Your breath is always present. Always listening," restorative yoga teacher Jillian Pransky writes in *Deep Listening*.[3] That I feel in the depths of my being—I am blessed to have many friends in this world, but none as abiding and generous as my own breath.

Controlled breathing also can help those suffering with depression interrupt the body/mind feedback loop—the mind has a thought, which brings up an emotion, which brings up a sensation in the body, which then brings up a thought and another emotion, which triggers more sensations and reactions in the body. It's no surprise that the book *The Mindful Way Through Depression,* coauthored by meditation pioneer Jon Kabat-Zinn, includes twenty-five references to using the breath for various aspects of dealing with depression.[4]

Mindfulness, Meditation, and the Brain

Kabat-Zinn is a researcher, author, and clinician who developed the practice of mindfulness-based stress reduction (MBSR), a technique I have studied and practiced. MBSR helps people cultivate awareness of themselves through practices such as gentle movement, body scans, and seated meditations, repeatedly coming back to the present moment in a nonjudgmental way.

Kabat-Zinn is one of many clinicians who have studied the effects of mindfulness and meditation practices on the brain, and the findings are clear: mindfulness can help reduce stress, anxiety, depression, and other mood disorders. Research from Johns Hopkins indicates it rivals the effects of antidepressants. Mindfulness also has been shown to provide valuable assistance for those suffering from trauma, addiction, and neurological disorders such as Parkinson's disease. It literally changes the structure of the brain.

What it does for me personally is almost beyond words. Meditation has become, by far, the aspect of yoga I practice the most—and it is indeed a practice, just like learning to control the body and the breath. Sometimes it doesn't "work"—I can't seem to get the monkey mind to sit down and shut up, or my body is uncomfortable and I decide to call it quits, or I simply fall asleep. But I am always inspired to try again, even if I don't do it well, because the act of going behind my eyelids and losing myself in my Self is a particular kind of heaven.

By training the brain to stay in the here and now, I am less trapped by the mind's usual frettings, the ones that pull me to either ruminate over the past or nervously anticipate the future. And that's really the big point of everything I just told you about learning to regulate our bodies and our minds. That's why ancient yogis developed these methods—not so they could have six-pack abs or buns of steel, but so they could minimize distractions in order to meditate, because meditation is one of the most profound methods we have of helping us connect to ourselves. With less external input, we can interact less with the physical senses and thoughts of the mind, and when those fall away, we are left to simply be.

Be what, exactly? Well, I guess that brings us back to the million-dollar question.

Who Am I, Really?

"Who do you think you are?" You might hear that question differently in your head depending on how you've been raised.

Who do you think you are?

Who do you *think* you are?

Or perhaps it's been spat at you this way: *Who the fuck do you think YOU are?*

That last version is the ugly one, the stinging one, the one that can make you question your significance or very justification for existence. You really only need to hear it once for the seed of doubt and unworthiness to be planted; when heard repeatedly, especially during the precious and formative early years, it can completely undermine any inherent sense of value. Then you must intentionally build a new foundation to replace the one eroded by the power of a single question.

That's why I'm careful about the way I ask myself this question. I don't ever ask it the loathing way; instead I combine the first two options into: *Who* do you *think* you are? Posed that way, I am reminded the answer is one of chosen identity. It's a belief. Which means there are not necessarily right or wrong answers (though some are much more conducive to agency and courage than others).

I choose to believe what yoga philosophy teaches about the soul, that within each one of us is an eternal, indestructible, divine essence, separate from our body—our true Self. The Self, the soul, is entirely different from the "ego," or our personality, which reflects ambition, fear, desire—all the trappings of humanity.

Ego is everything you think you are but aren't; true Self is everything you truly are but may not yet believe.

Ego is everything you think you are but aren't; true Self is everything you truly are but may not yet believe. Ego is a slice of you that believes it's the whole pie; Self is the whole pie, all the food in the land, a spiritual sustenance that sustains itself. Ego is labels; Self is beyond name or category or even definition. All you fear is an extension of ego and what it thinks of itself; all there is that has nothing to fear is Self, because Self is not just okay with the Universe—it *is* the Universe.

When you're angry or jealous or insecure, that's ego. Driven by desire or opinions others may hold about you? Ego. Coming at life from the limited perspective of the embodied "I" without any sense of the bigger, cosmic picture? Ego, ego, ego.

Now, don't get me wrong. The ego is not all bad and the goal is not to eviscerate it. It is the basis for what you think, feel, say, do— all of which are necessary parts of the human existence. It's the mechanism through which you interact with the physical world around you. But it's also the part of you that suffers, through experiences like disappointment, comparison, unmet desire, insecurity, pain or illness in the body, attachment, avoidance.

You might refer to this part of you as your personality, identity, self-concept, conscious mind, or any number of names. Essentially, that's your self, with a lowercase s.

The more empowering seat is that of the Self.

And when you have the confidence to honor your deepest desires, it doesn't make you full of yourself. It makes you filled with your Self.

Atman and Brahman

In yoga, we call the Self *atman,* and it is the same divine essence that is the Universe, or "God" (called *Brahman*). Who we are, at our very essence, is divine—the stuff of God. Not "made by God" or "separate from God" but, like, *actual God.* (Or, Goddess, if you prefer.) Let that sink in for a moment. I'll wait.

And, it's the practice of yoga—all that moving around and learning how to control the breath so we can control the mind—that allows us to come back to the God within us. We get quiet. Still. We release, breath by breath, the seemingly never-ending *blah, blah, blah* of the chattering brain and all the voice of fear has to say about why we're not good enough and instead we come back to who we really, truly are. We "re-member," as my friend Jim Zartman says.

Just as we're free to choose how we view ourselves, we can apply that same choice to the concept of "God," or the Universe, spirit, creator, source, consciousness, father, mother—whatever you like to call it, if anything. For some of us, the idea of God is a guiding, steadying force. For others, it carries flashbacks of judgment or disappointment. For others still, it may be an entirely foreign concept: unknown, unexplored, a nonentity. Whatever it is, it is just that: a concept. An identity. *A chosen belief.* In the same way a chef creates a signature recipe or a director makes a film, you get to make the whole thing up to your liking! How fun and liberating is that?

You also get to choose how these two identities—your Self and any higher spirit—interact. Do they communicate? Work together toward a common goal? Laugh together at stupid dad jokes?

My personal construct of God looks something like this: genderless, but with very strong goddess/mother energy and a preference to be called "she"; far wiser than I am, but without being judgy, and she never rubs it in; direct in that way only a loving BFF can be; the calming counterpart to my hummingbird nature; and has known me before my first breath and will, still, long after my tits are in my oatmeal. (Best of all, she's got the kind of sense of humor that appreciates a sentence that contains the words "God," "tits," and "oatmeal.")

My version of God has my best interest at heart and reminds me, gently, when I'm showing up from my humanness and forgetting the part of me that's all stardust and other glowy stuff—which I do regularly, though much less regularly than before we became acquainted. She cheers when I figure something out, and never hesitates to give me a little pinch on the ass or an "atta girl" wink when I need some courage. She shows me new ways of seeing, and all I have to do is show up, be curious about what she knows that I don't yet, and be open to this existence, however it unfolds.

Another way of putting it, I suppose, is that she loves me purely and I trust her.

I am neither theologian nor evangelist; I am not trying to "convert" you to any particular way of thinking or set of beliefs. Those are yours and yours alone, chosen and cultivated by each individual. But think about it: every major religion was, at one early point, a set of beliefs that lived in one person's head. *Why can't that be the case for you and yours?*

> Think about it: every major religion was, at one early point, a set of beliefs that lived in one person's head. *Why can't that be the case for you and yours?*

Spirituality isn't science, where theories can be proven and disproven. It's not math, where numbers are facts and one correct answer renders everything else incorrect. I think it's a little more like art, where intention, meaning, and beauty are bestowed by the one creating it, and impact is felt by the one receiving it.

When it comes to personal faith, you are both the creator of your belief system and the one impacted by it.

I liken the consideration of different beliefs to shopping for a swimsuit: What complements one of us may not be right for another; what might look cute on the hanger may not be a fit for your unique curves and contours. But you won't know that until you try it on.

Here's what my spiritual swimsuit looks like: supportive enough to keep me together, yet loose enough that I am exquisitely comfortable. I'm not constricted, but I'm not flopping around, either. It protects my most vulnerable parts while allowing the sun of life to warm my skin. In this garment, I am free and at peace in my Self.

You, however, might want a little more structure, or for it to reveal less, or reflect a different color. So don't feel like you have to wear *my* swimsuit; you can keep shopping until you find one that's good enough, or custom design one that is just for you.

The point is, it's entirely your call.

The Voice of Your Soul

We already know about one voice inside of you: the Pipsqueak Twerp, the voice of your ego. Is there also a voice of your soul, that ageless and fearless and indestructible part at your center, the part of you that *is God*?

I believe there is, and it's a voice I like. A lot. It's the still voice of the Universe. The quiet whisper of knowing. The sound of your otherworldly inner refuge, made of spirit, that is inherently perfect and sacred and noble. The voice of your grace and light and goodness and possibility. The voice of the *real* you.

This is the voice of Choice, not Fear.

This is the voice of your divinity.

What's spectacularly cool about divinity is that the presence of divinity *inside* means we are special and powerful, and divinity *outside* means we also are held by something special and powerful. I think of that idea, of being held, when I look at the words inked on the inside of my right forearm: *How bold one is when one is sure of being loved.* (I can't take credit for the phrase—it's Freud—though I did tweak it a bit. The original phrase is "How bold one *gets* . . ." but I much prefer the idea of *being* bold as a regular state rather than just becoming it once.)

There is room for personal interpretation, of course, when it comes to who is doing the loving. Maybe we're loved by God, like we've talked about. Perhaps it's a lover. Or maybe Freud was talking about Self-love. Maybe he meant all three, I can't say—but because that's the option I like best, it is the one I choose to adopt. And, I pay it forward.

If you believe—in the very deepest center of your being— that you are loved, then I'm hoping you also will . . .

. . . assume that being loved means you are inherently worthy of that love, and if you are worthy of that love . . .

. . . then maybe you aren't actually all those shitty things the voice in your head says about your weight and your looks and your smarts and your abilities and your entire future . . .

. . . and maybe you can realize that just about everything that Pipsqueak Twerp has to say is nothing but complete and utter bullshit . . .

. . . then perhaps you can let go of all the things you aren't and instead tune in to the still, soft voice within, the one that speaks the truth of your divinity . . .

. . . and, instead of being afraid, you can be confident and bold and do daring things.

You follow my logic? You see where it starts? It starts back with that notion of being held by something bigger than you.

Maybe you're not at a place in life where you want to say "God." That's okay. Maybe the love you feel comes through a friend or sister or a parent or a lover or a pet or even a memory. Wherever it may come from, it is there, I assure you. And the beauty of developing a relationship with your own brave, indestructible, ego-less, God-like, true Self is that 24/7, 365 days a year, it will *always* be there for you to lean on.

That, my friends, is the real power of yoga—not a handstand, not a great pic on the beach at sunset for Instagram—but the bringing together of your divine spirit with that same divinity of the entire universe . . . the same divinity that's in every person, every blade of grass, every drop in the ocean . . . the same divinity that's not afraid.

In the wise words that trace back, best as I can tell, to a dude on Twitter who used to go by the handle @Porkbeard: "You're a ghost driving a meat-coated skeleton made from stardust. What do you have to be scared of?"

> **"You're a ghost driving a meat-coated skeleton made from stardust. What do you have to be scared of?"**
> —@Porkbeard

Looking at the world in this way sure put into different perspective my old concerns over the "temporary" aspects of existence like fear over leaving a no-good job or a worn-out relationship. That fear was understandable for Ego-Driven Becky, who hadn't yet learned what kind of magic she was made of.

But Stardust Becky? Divine Becky? The one who breathes in the connection to her Self and breathes out all the BS that *isn't* that? She tends to look at things differently because she's got the power of the Universe within her. Stardust Becky is badass and bold, with enormous capacity for choice and change.

I hope you can see that you are badass, bold, and backed by the power of the Universe, too.

Closing Exercise: *Exploring the Divinity Within*

What is "God" to you? Do you believe there is divinity around you? Within you? Do you hear that still, small voice? Explain. What does being loved mean to you? Who holds you—a lover, a friend, a power greater than that of any human? The divinity within? How does believing that you are held shift your feelings about fear and courage and being brave enough to make the choices you need for the life you want? How can an assurance of being fundamentally loved, simply because you exist and you are divine, empower you? Describe what you believe—or, what you would like to believe. Remember, this part is entirely up to you.

6

The Power of Soul-Guided Choices

Make the voice of your wish louder than the voice of your habit.
   —Elena Brower

Most people believe that the opposite of fear is courage. I believe the opposite of fear is *choice*—especially when we choose not from the brain, but from our stardust selves.

When we make decisions that are backed by our inherent divinity rather than from our ego-driven fears, we bring into being the confidence, peace, and freedom we so desperately seek.

When the Soul Speaks

A funny thing happened right after I left corporate America: with all the pressure lifted, my mothering heart satisfied and full, and boundless possibility ahead, my drinking actually *sky-rocketed*. Without the demand to be constantly alert, accessible, or productive, I was able to slide in to my best-loved pastime—day drinking—partly because I kept it well-hidden, but partly because this time was the dawn of the bullshit "mommy juice" culture and I had two little girls. For what felt like the first time in my life, *I fit right in.*

No one knew my tumbler on a hot day with the kids at the community pool wasn't filled with iced tea but rather coconut vodka with limeade. And, if they did, no one cared because we all bought into the idea that a mother needed alcohol to cope with her children. (Is it any surprise that the weekly after-school gatherings I had with a few of the other kindergarten moms were dubbed "Boozy Tuesdays"?)

Despite my desire to be present, I was more gone than ever and so far outside of my integrity and what I wanted for myself and my family that it physically hurt. Twenty-five years of drinking had taken parts of me I thought I might never reclaim.

Thankfully, divine intervention struck in the form of one of my favorite yoga teachers, Elena Brower. During a moment of stillness in a weekend workshop, Elena asked us to look at our lives through the lens of lineage and identify one aspect of our personality, our way of being, that we didn't particularly like but nonetheless carried forward from the past.

The voice in my head pierced the otherwise silent room, thundering before the sentence had fully left her mouth: *You drink too much!* Tears spilled out from behind my closed eyes.

In those four words, there was no hint of the telltale inflection that marks a question, only the certainty of fact, the inarguable power of declaration in the form of a roar. I sobbed in shameful knowing, too overtaken by the depth of the startling to care what the hundred other people around might make of my tears. Despite knowing firsthand the pain my father's drinking had caused, and what it had cost our family, I had followed in his footsteps and carried alcohol abuse into the next generation's experience. *Monkey see, monkey do.*

What made the moment of my inner shout so powerful, so *pivotal*, was that I instinctively recognized the voice of the bellow, even though I'd never heard it before. The tone was native, inherent, the feeling in my mortal chest a mystery that I innately understood. It was not my brain telling me to stop; it was *my soul*. It was the infinite me, the stardust within my meat-coated skeleton. And with that primal scream, I took the first tender steps toward the woman I would become.

A couple hours later I met Dave out for lunch. It was the day after our tenth wedding anniversary (two years before our divorce), the girls were spending the night at my mother's, and we were celebrating. After two rounds of Bloody Marys and a glass of Zinfandel halfway gone, I brought up the experience with Elena at the yoga workshop.

"She told us to take that thing we brought forward from the past—that thing we do but wish we didn't—and hold it in our hands, as gentle as we might a little kitten. And then she told us to lift it up and let it go." I choked out the words, tears falling onto the table below as I raised my arms in demonstration.

I came clean that I had been drinking more—and struggling more—than I had let on over the years, that my many failed attempts at giving up alcohol as a New Year's resolution were not as innocuous as they seemed, that I was deeply ashamed of my inability to moderate or limit or really have any sense of control over alcohol whatsoever. I felt like I was the puppet and alcohol was pulling the strings.

I can't do it by myself, I wailed in acknowledgment before asking if he would stop with me.

That good man, bless him, didn't hesitate a second: "Of course."

At that, terror rumbled in my guts and bowels. My breath stopped. All of this truth being dealt with outside of my body, in the sunlight, rather than in the confines of my own head where no one could force accountability on me, felt like an awful yet hopeful relief. I wanted to back myself fully into the corner and somehow run like hell at the same time.

Are we really going to do this? I asked my soul, blinking back tears, followed by *Holy fuck, what have I done?*

"Okay," I exhaled long and slow, praying that the absence of air would restart my breath. "Let's go home and cook those fancy steaks and open that special bottle of Cab we brought back from Napa like we planned, and then tomorrow, no more."

Dave looked down at the mostly empty glasses on the table. "Nope," he said. "You've already had your last drink."

Jesus, I thought and, possibly for the first time ever, I walked away from liquid still in the glass. *Is this what it feels like to feel the fear and do it anyway?*

Preya and Shreya

The first days of not drinking were nervous and miserable. Same for the first weeks and first months.

Just before bed each night, as I would put the day's dishes in the dishwasher and turn out the kitchen light, I'd mark another notch on the calendar that hung inside the pantry door. Time seemed to go molasses slow in the beginning; some days I'd visit that calendar multiple times just to make sure I hadn't missed something. *Nope. Still fucking Tuesday.*

After a while, though, I went to it less frequently. Some nights I even crossed off two dry days in a row! After nine months or so, I stopped counting days altogether. But let me tell you something: I still count the years. I will forever count these miraculous sober years.

Two ideas from yoga helped get my head to the pillow each night without a drink.

First was *the chosen knowing* of my own divinity; the deep belief that, because I am God, it was my duty to honor the holiness within me. In fact, "honor the holy" was my mantra that whole year.

Second was the concept of *preya* and *shreya,* my favorite part of yoga philosophy and one I wish more people knew.

There is no English equivalent for these Sanskrit terms, but you can think of them essentially as instant gratification versus long-term fulfillment. *Preya* is what's good and easy and pleasing; *shreya* is beneficial and takes the long view. *Preya* is quick, often fleeting, enjoyment; *shreya* is lasting and leads us closer to enduring contentment. *Preya* is a quart of ice cream; *shreya* is eating your metaphorical vegetables. You can guess which of the two paths, always present and competing against one another for our attention, gets picked more often in our modern society.

This idea of these two opposing paths for choice underpins

one of the more memorable metaphors I've come across: the description of the Self as the rider in a chariot. In his book *Essence of the Upanishads: A Key to Indian Spirituality,* the teacher Eknath Easwaran describes it this way:

> Your body is the chariot, drawn by five powerful horses: the senses [sight, sound, taste, smell, and touch]. These horses travel not so much through space as time. They gallop, let us say, from birth towards death, pursuing the objects of their desire. The discriminating intellect—judgment—is the driver, whose job it is to see clearly and not drive you over a cliff. His reins are the mind, your emotions and desires. And you are the rider—the Self.
>
> . . . once these powerful horses are trained, they are as responsive as show horses. Imagine having strong, sensitive senses with a clear, discriminating intellect holding the reins. If the taste buds start to drag you away, you just give a tug on the will and all the senses understand. This is expert driving, and perfect living, too. When the senses are trained, you can go anywhere and never lose your capacity to choose.
>
> . . . But there is a rub. When our horses want something not particularly beneficial—say, a martini—which of us can exercise our authority and say, "How about some lemonade, instead?" The horses will smile to themselves and drop us off at the Happy Hour anyway. "I've got an alcohol problem," we explain. "Not at all," [God] would reply. "Your horses have an alcohol problem. You have a horse problem. You'd better get them trained."[1]

As someone who did, in fact, have a horse problem, this passage still lands like a dart in the bullseye of my heart.

In the early days of my sobriety, I would close my eyes and visualize the strong craving in my senses as a stampede of horses running . . . well, nowhere. Because that is where a return to drinking would have taken me: *nowhere*.

Nowhere good, anyway.

To pick up a drink would be, as it always had been, pure *preya*—just another empty, temporary fix—when what I needed was the long-term healing made in the name of *shreya*. What I needed in sobriety was simple: to choose from my soul rather than my fear.

When I think about *shreya*, I'm reminded of what Brené Brown says about integrity: "Integrity is choosing courage over comfort; choosing what is right over what is fun, fast, or easy; and choosing to practice our values rather than simply professing them."[2]

Preya, to put it in that language, is fun, fast, and easy. *Shreya* chooses courage over comfort. *Shreya* practices your values rather than simply professing them.

I invite you to take a moment here to reflect on the big areas of your life and consider: Are you tempted by the quick, easy gratification of *preya*, or are you guided by the beneficial long view of *shreya*? Do you routinely take the easy way out, or are you willing to risk some immediate discomfort for long-term growth?

Here are some questions to get you thinking. After you contemplate them honestly, I encourage you to look for the patterns in your answers.

Work

- Do you enjoy your work/career? Does it fulfill you?
- Does your work conflict or align with your values and ethics?
- Is your compensation in line with your experience and contributions, or are you paid less than your worth?
- Do you advocate for yourself when it comes to work-life flexibility and balance?
- Do you feel valued and appreciated for your contributions?
- Is there room for growth?

Finances

- Do you have, and live by, a budget?
- Do you typically pay your bills on time?
- What kind of debt do you carry?
- How much do you save in proportion to how much you spend?
- How often do you engage in "retail therapy"?

Relationships with Others

- Are you comfortable setting and sticking to boundaries with friends, family, coworkers, and others who ask of your time, energy, and attention?

- Do you tell white lies, avoid specific people, or go along with things even if they contradict your values in order to avoid confrontation—or are you practiced in the art of courageous conversations?
- Are you treated with integrity, kindness, and compassion?
- Do you receive as much from your relationships as you give to them?

Physical Health

- Do you make and keep preventative and as-needed appointments with your general practitioner, dentist, eye doctor, OB-GYN, etc. (as applicable)?
- Do you tend to ignore or "power through" your body's aches, pains, illnesses, and conditions?
- How often do you eat fast or relatively unhealthy food compared to foods you know are healthier?
- How regularly do you drink soda, caffeine, high-calorie drinks?
- Do you use (or abuse) alcohol or drugs?
- Do you exercise?

Inner Life

- Do you work (or have you worked) with a mental health professional? Are diagnosed conditions treated appropriately?
- Do you have a mindfulness or meditation practice?

- Do you believe in or have relationship with any kind of "higher power"?
- Do you engage in activities such as journaling, spending time in nature, or making time for reflection or solitude?

Getting Off Autopilot

Once you become familiar with the concepts of *preya* and *shreya*, it is easy to spot their influence in your daily life; you just have to keep your eyes open for the patterns and be willing to turn off the autopilot when you see it's not taking you in the right direction.

Autopilot is the enemy of boldness, because autopilot equals tunnel vision.

When you operate on autopilot, you reflexively do the same things, over and over, because you haven't paused long enough to consider a more conscious choice. On autopilot, you can access just a narrow slice of the possibilities around you. In fact, the aperture is so narrow that you become literally blind to the options. You're being carried by habit, by momentum, rather than going where you intentionally point your headlights. Hell, on autopilot, you don't even need to check whether you even *have* headlights, because you're not actually driving. You're just drifting.

But when you get more intentional about the choices you make—no matter how small or seemingly inconsequential—the lens through which you view those choices begins to open up. The realm of what is possible widens and you can see just how many more chances life offers to align to your preferences and values, through your discernment, to your deeper being.

> **Change starts with acknowledging the life you're living doesn't line up with the life you want. From there, it's about getting off autopilot.**

Change starts with acknowledging the life you're living doesn't line up with the life you want. From there, it's about getting off autopilot. Then you can make decisions that honor and support that most holy part within you.

Choosing from Your Soul

Often, we go into the change-seeking process anticipating the need for an act of courage/drama/cord-cutting a la Thelma and Louise. What I typically see happen, though, is the realization that smaller-scale, more personalized choices can yield more clarity, transformation, and, ultimately, long-term contentment than driving off a cliff.

One of the sweetest examples of this involves a young man who attended one of my earliest workshops. When he first walked in to the yoga studio that Saturday afternoon with his girlfriend, I remember being surprised just by the look of him: where everyone else was a woman somewhere between their mid-thirties to early sixties, he couldn't have been more than twenty. Just a kid.

While the middle-aged ladies waited on their mats in their comfy yoga, lounge, or otherwise stretchy clothes, the young man's grease-stained jeans—along with the light air of oil mixed with sweat that followed him in—made clear that he came straight from work at a gas station or auto repair shop. When he removed his steel-toed work boots, the bottoms of his dingy, hole-pocked white socks carried the dirty imprint of his foot. He may have looked out of place, but I recall being so impressed with how comfortable he seemed in his own skin. For the next three hours, he participated in everything the workshop threw at him: the yoga poses he had never before attempted, the quiet meditation time, the journal prompts. He didn't say much, but he was clearly present.

Toward the end of the session, as we went around the room and participants shared what first step they planned to take as part of their effort to make a change in their life, the young man blew us all away with his simple, yet profound declaration: "I'm going to call my mom," he said. "I haven't talked to her in a year, but as soon as I leave here I'm going to find a payphone and call."

I was not the only one who teared up then. Because soul-guided choices don't need to be flashy to be bold. They just need to be yours.

> Because soul-guided choices don't need to be flashy to be bold. They just need to be yours.

Here are a few other examples of the soul-guided choices I've seen folks make as a result of doing the work of getting aligned with their deeper selves:

- Linda thought her job was *the* "not this" keeping her stuck and, in some ways, she came looking for permission to quit after years of misery and handwringing. What she got instead was the encouragement to trust her own inner wisdom and, from that place, use her voice to speak her needs. Once empowered by that shift, which she attributes in large part to a year of soaking up the goodness that comes with dedicated yoga practice, the decision to return to her hometown and leave the job was an easy, intuitive one. Clarity replaced doubt, a sense of her power within began to overshadow a lifetime of insecurity, and Linda was able to begin a different life—different not because of what she did for a living, but because of how she showed up in it. "My life didn't have space for anything else, but it was so empty," she told me later. "Now, it's more full than I ever could have imagined."

- Felicia was a successful, established, in-demand attorney. As she eyed retirement, she wondered whether she should say goodbye not only to her job but, for the sake of an entirely fresh start, to her longtime partner, too. After focusing on her values, fears, and deepest longings, she surprised the class on our last day with . . . a wedding announcement! "I'm seventy-one and my partner is seventy-four and we have been engaged for twenty-one years. I realize that everything I want, it's all right here in front of my face. So you know what we're gonna do?! We're getting married!" she told the group over Zoom. There wasn't a dry eye in the house.

- Tammi was someone who tended to alternate between hanging out in the shadows and cautiously, nervously, stepping into the light; her deepest fear was that if someone saw the "real" her, they wouldn't like what they saw. As she began to not just acknowledge but really embrace her true divine nature, she made the conscious and often uncomfortable choice to allow herself to be more fully seen. By revealing her more vulnerable side, rather than relying on the defense mechanism of projecting strength from a distance, Tammi became a magnet for more openness and authenticity in her relationships with others. She also learned that when she allowed people to see the real her, they actually *loved* what they saw! In the coming years, Tammi received professional and other connection opportunities that capitalized on her special openness and, through the simple act of saying "yes," her life shifted in myriad ways. And, by continuing to allow her light to shine, Tammi now helps other people reveal *themselves* in ways that are expansive and healing.

The common thread weaving through each of these stories is the deeply human ache, one so buried it isn't always visible to the naked eye, that begs: *See me. Hear me. Know me. The real me.* Not the "me" who performs, or shapeshifts to conform, or minimizes her feelings or needs to fit in and keep the peace, or denies her truth to make others more comfortable—but the one who simply *is,* as she is. Only when this fundamental yearning for authenticity is acknowledged, and the spirit that has been trying to break free from the inside out is let loose, can we step into the promise of our true Self.

I know how it feels when the soul is ignored because I lived that way for too long—cold-shouldering my inner knowing when it came to work, marriage, decades of alcoholic drinking—all because I didn't know how to speak her tongue. I gave too much weight to Other People's expectations, allowing "shoulds" to override "wants." Man, those ingrained habits are hard to unwind.

Listening to the voice of the soul is what this whole life thing is about, and learning to do it is the essence of the human experience.

> Listening to the voice of the soul is what this whole life thing is about, and learning to do it is the essence of the human experience.

We are not here to be walking revenue generators or codependent people pleasers or arbitrary line toe-ers or even upstanding citizens (remember: *human beings,* not *human doings*). We are here to connect our souls with understanding, with meaning, with compassion and contribution, with learning and evolution, with joy. How that manifests—what shape it takes, how it's defined—is for each one of us to decide for ourselves. We get to measure the success of our chosen existence not by how it looks, but by how it feels.

We do not arrive at this place by accident, though; this freedom of a life based on our own personal values and priorities, based on the guidance of our deepest knowing, is one we must intentionally choose. And that chosen life begins with the willingness to confront fear and change that which needs to be changed.

Do you know what that is? Can you feel what inside you needs to shift so that the life you're living lines up with the life you want, rather than the life you feel stuck in? Are you ready and willing to make soul-guided choices?

If your answer is a clear, bellowing *YES!* . . . grab on to that. If it's a faint, faraway *I don't know* . . . keep listening. If there are not answers yet but perhaps a word vomit of questions, or hot tears, or the ache that will not stop tugging on your sleeve . . . pay attention. Don't be afraid. Suppressing, avoiding, tuning out gets you nowhere. Look your Self in the eye instead.

Remember, the opposite of fear isn't just courage.

The opposite of fear is choice.

Closing Exercise: *Getting Off Autopilot*

I invite you here to pause and consider your life's journey thus far, looking close in at first and then widening the aperture to see the bigger picture:

- What do you currently do mindlessly, habitually, reflexively that you would like to change? As Elena Brower challenged me to think all those years ago, are there any habits from your lineage you perpetuate, perhaps despite your better intentions?
- When it comes to the areas of your life where you feel the most heartburn, have you arrived at your current situation by design—or because you have been, knowingly or not, on autopilot?
- Finally, what bold decision do you need to make in order to get off autopilot and create the life you most deeply desire? What needs to change?

Remember, "bold" doesn't necessarily translate to "drastic." As my tattoo reads: *How bold one is when one is sure of being loved.* What change will allow you to love and honor your Self more, to let your soul be free?

Please be excruciatingly honest and direct here, especially if this feels overwhelming. Say the thing you may never have said before. Now is not the time to conceal anything, especially from your own curious eyes. As the writer Jeff Brown notes: "We have nothing to hide and nowhere to hide it."[3]

7

Trade-Offs, Consequences, and Boundaries

Don't worry if you're making waves just by being yourself; the moon does it all the time.
   —Scott Stabile

Rewind, if you will, to that moment on the beach in San Francisco when I sobbed to my friend Chelsey about how fiercely, how desperately I wanted to be living a different life. Once she dropped the hot bomb of permission— "If you're that unhappy doing what you're doing, then do something different. And if that doesn't work out, do something different again."—I started to get excited. Like, *really* excited. Like, *let's fucking go!* excited.

We continued talking about it as we walked down the beach, across the bluster of the Golden Gate Bridge, and all the way to sleepy Sausalito—covering a lot of literal and metaphorical ground along the way. We stopped in a waterside restaurant, ordered lunch, and settled our worn-out bodies at a sunny table outside. As I looked south in the direction from which we had come, I knew I was ready. I took a deep breath and dialed Dave back in St. Louis to declare, once and for all, that the hand-wringing was over.

I was ready to quit my job.

"You want to do *what* to your *what*?!" he replied.

I shared with him the aha moment from the beach and said I was resolute. "Okayyyy," he said slowly. "Why don't you come home, we'll put it down on paper, see what it looks like, and then decide?"

That seemed reasonable—but, lacking the patience to wait three more excruciating days to get started, I began my calculations immediately. First was a balance sheet of material pros and cons, essentially a showdown between time and money that required a verdict on which one I valued more at that point in my life.

The money piece required a deeper dive, especially the sacrifices that we, as a family, would need to make in order to make the house payment on one salary. *Goodbye, Coach bags and the fancy suits I was tired of wearing anyway. Adios, dinners out and cable TV. So long, kids' college fund and vacations on airplanes. 401(k)? What's a 401(k)??* (Ten years later and I'm still trying to remember the answer to *that* little question.)

The next considerations—the what-ifs—were the biggies, because they were the ones I couldn't *know* the answers to. Best I could do was make an educated guess and hope I was right—and, if I was wrong, be willing to live with it. *Would the door be open if I changed my mind and wanted to go back? Would exiting the freeway of fast-track career development mean difficulty getting back on later if I so chose?* And, a question that, in retrospect, I wish I'd spent more time with: *Was my marriage strong and stable enough to withstand the shift?*

The next morning, I called Dave again to make my case with more urgency. "I've done the assessment and believe with my whole heart we can make this work. What I need from you is to hold my hand and take this leap of faith."

I could hear him gulp from two thousand miles away. "Okay," he said quietly. And two days later, mere hours after I landed back home in St. Louis, I exhaled all the tension in my body and offered my resignation.

A few years later, a friend wrote and asked whether I ever missed the hustle and bustle of that old corporate job. My initial response: "Hmmmmm . . . let me think . . . um . . . nope!" And then I expanded in a stream of consciousness that reinforced just how right my decision was.

"I miss seeing some folks every day. I miss my paycheck. I *really* miss my health insurance benefits. Occasionally I miss a night alone in a hotel room.

"I do not miss feeling crushed by a never-ending burden of stress. I do not miss eating lunch hunched over my computer every day. I do not miss high heels. I do not miss billing or time entry or forecasts or margins. I do not miss measuring my worth by my title. I do not miss dreading Sunday nights and Monday mornings.

"Now I love waking up. I love setting my own agenda based on my own priorities and values. I love that taking time out of my day to unroll my yoga mat is considered 'professional development.' I love flip-flops. I love wearing my hair curly. I love being my own boss and having the freedom to chase any damn dream I choose—with no one telling me I can't. I love spending more time with my kids. I love spending more time with *me*. I love feeling myself evolve in ways I never expected.

"Do I get stressed about the long-term financial implications of walking away from six figures for a less-certain future? Sure, sometimes. But do I question whether I did the right thing? Not for a second. As a good friend reminds me, 'Shit works out.'"

Of course, change does not happen in a vacuum.

Every decision has an effect, whether you think of it in terms of echoes or ripples, results or outcomes, ramifications or repercussions. There can be upshots and payoffs and spin-offs, fallout and backlash, eventualities and inevitabilities. Doors open, doors close. And the people around you *will* respond in some way, meaning there will be opinions to consider, roadblocks to navigate, subsequent choices to make.

You want to leave the company where you have logged years and are a known quantity? *Well, you'll have to be the new kid who must prove herself somewhere else.* Thinking of putting some distance between you and a member of your friend circle? *Beware: it may cost you multiple relationships if others pick sides.* Ready to explore the roots of your mental and emotional suffering? *Careful, now. There are gonna be some creepy crawlies down there to contend with.*

Newton's third law of motion—"For every action, there is an equal and opposite reaction"—is relevant here, particularly if you replace "action/reaction" with words such as "force" or "energy." And while you cannot possibly predict every resistance, you can anticipate many of the most likely trade-offs and consequences, which I will tell you from experience tend to hurt much less if they are considered before a choice is made rather than after the fact.

Stakeholders and Scenarios

When I worked in PR, one of the parts of my job I enjoyed most was scenario planning and risk management. (Seems fitting for the child of two insurance agents, yes?) This involved anticipating crises that were likely to arise as part of a company's day-to-day business (think customer and employee issues, regulatory and legislative concerns, accidents and natural disasters, etc.) and then preparing a thoughtful, strategic action/communication protocol to guide the response. (For example, workers at a company's plant are preparing to strike. What should the company be prepared to do, not do, say, not say, to employees, to investors, the community, the news media, etc.? If the union does *xyz*, how will the company respond?)

I believe this same kind of strategic planning must be incorporated in the consideration of soul-guided choices, especially to avoid being blindsided by the natural consequences and considerations that can arise from your decision-making. You may ultimately decide to plow forward, *consequences be damned!*, but at least give yourself the gift of going in with eyes wide open.

Because, let's be real here: just because you're inspired by your soul doesn't mean you throw all your smarts out the window.

There are four major areas of life I recommend considering as part of the choice-making process, as these are the ones most likely to be affected by whatever it is you decide to do next. (Note: "Affected" doesn't necessarily mean "lost" or "ruined" or otherwise impacted negatively; "affected" also could translate to "bolstered," "enriched," "balanced out," "released," "redirected," "energized," "neutralized," "disentangled." Some ripple effects are quite positive.)

- **Finances:** What are the financial implications of this choice, both positive and negative? Are they so severe that the choice is untenable or, conversely, so incredible that you can't say no? What are you willing to live with, or without? Where does financial security rank within your value system?

- **Time and energy:** If you invest more *here,* what might you need to sacrifice over *there*? If you can save it *here,* where else might you spend it? What are you willing to do—or not do—to pursue this goal? Who, or what, deserves the best/most/least of what you have to give?

- **Relationships and family dynamics:** Who are the most valued stakeholders in your life (partner, children, coworkers, family, community, etc?), and to what degree will their needs and opinions influence this situation? How much do you need their approval/ support? Can you withstand their explicit disapproval, lack of support, or unhappiness with your choice? How might your choice/change impact your most important relationships?

- **Personal development:** What are the implications for your physical and mental health? For your spiritual growth? And where do those things rank in priority? In what way could this change either trigger or alleviate some of your character watchouts (such as perfectionism, insecurity, or codependency)? Will this change ultimately cause you to grow or to suffer? Will it bring you closer to your values and true Self or further away? What are you willing to endure or sacrifice in the short term?

If/Then/And

After identifying your most important stakeholders and the areas of your life most likely to be touched by the choice you are considering, I invite you to go through an exercise I call "If/Then/And": *If _____ happens, then I'll likely _____, and ultimately, I will _____.*

To illustrate how it works, I'll share the kinds of scenarios, trade-offs, and consequences I considered as Dave and I moved toward our divorce—some practical, some emotional—and the determinations I made that informed how, ultimately, I would proceed. You may see some of your own considerations reflected here, even if the larger question you're contemplating is completely different. (And, if not, you'll find a blank template at the end of this chapter.) Regardless of the nature of the choice you face, the framework for thinking through these aspects of your life is applicable.

If . . .	Then . . .	And
Finances dictate that I won't be able to stay in this home unless I go back to a traditional job . . .	. . . I will lose this place I love, the one within walking distance of the girls' school, the one with all the memories, the one I have worked so hard to cultivate, the one I thought I'd grow old in . . .	Since Dave has decided to stay within the school district boundaries, I am willing to downsize to a much smaller home in a less pricey neighborhood with a more modest lifestyle for the sake of inner peace, a fresh start, and pursuing my dream of growing *You Are Not Stuck*. I will live within my means without going back to my old way of life in order to afford my old luxuries. My guiding mantra: Home is anywhere you're loved. It doesn't have to be fancy.
The girls have a hard time coping with the emotional disruption of divorce . . .	. . . it will break my heart to watch them experience a situation they didn't ask for and won't understand. I don't know if I can put them through the short-term pain or the long-term impact . . .	Sadly, what the girls will have to process will be real and significant—but it cannot keep us from doing what we both know must be done. Dave and I have demonstrated a sincere willingness to part in friendship and with grace, and we are committed to investing the time, money, and emotional bandwidth required to help the girls process the pain and loss that comes with divorce.

Our friends feel the need to "pick sides" . . .	. . . the best we can do is show, through our continued friendship, that our decision was mutual and it would be unnecessary for anyone to have to show loyalty to one of us over the other . . .	I recognize that some friendships will naturally fall away once Dave and I are no longer a couple, and I accept that as a part of the process.
I find myself divorced (for the second time!) at age 40 . . .	. . . it's possible I'll wind up a decrepit old spinster who will never be loved again . . .	If being alone is my fate, so be it. I would rather be at peace with myself and live alone than feel desperately lonely while living in a shell of a relationship. Remember: Home is anyplace you are loved— which means home is *within me*. (Also, I am not willing to concede that I have been kissed for the last time.)

I want to stress that there is an enormous difference between "scenario planning" and "future tripping." While scenario planning does require some imagination, it stops short of rumination over things that (1) you cannot control, and (2) may never come to pass.

Looking too far into the future is like trying to predict what will happen a thousand steps from now, forgetting that the steps will look more like a drunken cowboy doing a do-si-do on a zig-zag roller coaster than a peaceful monk gliding down a quiet hallway.

Life, like learning and growing and healing, is not linear.

Boundaries

Once you have identified the likely consequences of your choice and the trade-offs and sacrifices you are willing to accept, you will have lots of opportunities to stand by your decisions. It's almost as if the Universe will place you in situations that force you—not through your words but through your actions—to affirm your choice.

Broke? Let me tempt you with the prospect of this vacation you can't afford!

Adopting a healthier eating regimen? Here's some birthday cake!

Working on a clean break from your ex? Well, well, well, look who just walked in to Thanksgiving dinner at your mother's house.

Talked with your boss for better work-life balance? I know it's Friday at 4 P.M. but we need you to unfuck this giant, gnarly hairball just one more time.

I come back here to Elizabeth Gilbert's question: "What are you willing to do to have the life you say you want?" That's because soul-guided choices often are about more than what we are willing to *do,* but also what we are willing *not to do,* what we are willing to say or not say, what we allow and what we refuse, which bonds we sever and which ones we strengthen, what we choose to explore and what is better to ignore, what we will endure and what we will relinquish. And, because all of these considerations don't exist in a vacuum, you can see it is within the context of our relationships with others that we will experience the most friction around the soul-guided choices we make for ourselves.

Enter boundaries.

In her bestselling book *Set Boundaries, Find Peace*, therapist Nedra Glover Tawwab defines boundaries as "expectations and needs that help you feel safe and comfortable in your relationships"—and if there ever was a time you needed to feel secure in your relationships with others, let me assure you it is now.

Tawwab points to six types of boundaries—physical, sexual, intellectual, emotional, material, and time—and says the cost of not having healthy boundaries includes people-pleasing and prioritizing others' needs above your own, feeling unheard and unappreciated, and experiencing stress, burnout, resentment, anxiety, and depression.[1] How can we possibly move toward our soul's deepest longing if we are bogged down by all of this?

Change is difficult enough; having good boundaries makes it easier.

No, I can't afford to go on that trip right now; please don't try to talk me into it.

Happy birthday, darling, but I'll pass on the cake.

Mom, I wasn't aware so-and-so was coming and I'm very uncomfortable; see you at Christmas.

Sorry, boss, I have firm plans and can't take on that last-minute project this weekend. But I'll jump in first thing Monday.

As clean and effortless as those responses may sound, they can feel disastrously messy and require great effort—especially early on, when you are unpracticed. Still, setting and enforcing boundaries that protect your decisions is an imperative component to moving forward with any sort of success—which, you will recall, you get to define by the metrics of your choosing—even if that means getting feedback that isn't always intended as a compliment.

"You've Changed"

Ever heard that one before? Sometimes folks will notice the way you've shifted things and they'll mean that nicely—although, just as often, they mean something else.

Important people in your life may, for whatever reason, hold on to the "old" you. Perhaps they feel safer with the person they knew instead of the one they don't yet fully comprehend. Maybe hanging on to the past makes them more comfortable about themselves. Maybe they simply don't like the new version.

And that's okay.

That's not up to you to decide, or even understand.

It's only up to you to accept.

I feel a pang of this sometimes when I look back to my former life, when the focus was almost unequivocally on work. My job directed everything: my attention, my energy, my circle of friends, even how I felt about myself in non-work hours (the few it seemed there were). It consumed my whole world. My identity was completely wrapped up in it.

When I shifted gears all those years ago, it may have appeared to some to be fairly drastic, perhaps even out of character. I mean, who morphs practically overnight from a tightly wound, success-chasing, clients-come-first, don't-take-no-for-an-answer chick with sleek hair and power heels into a barefoot, curly-haired, airy-fairy yoga teacher content to just sit around with her breath and her thoughts and her notebooks? Me, that's who! (And, thankfully, lots of other folks, too.)

But I felt judged in some way . . . almost as if those I had "left behind" took my personal choice as a condemnation of theirs, that my decision to leave somehow was a blatant criticism of their desire to stay.

I felt that eyebrow-raising, too, when I first got sober. Like work, drinking had been an integral part of my identity. I wasn't quite sure who I'd be without it—but I knew for certain that I needed to find out.

I noticed in those early months the news that I'd quit drinking elicited one of three responses, with no direct prompting from me:

1. People were inspired to look hard at—and, ultimately, change—their own habits.
2. People's defensiveness about their own habits moved to offense when they proactively said something to the effect of, "Well, don't think this means *I'm* going to change anything."
3. People fell away quietly.

It's funny how switching directions and then enforcing the boundaries we need to be successful can come at the expense of relationships—especially the ones we thought were rock-solid, the ones that were a foundational part of our identities, the ones we expected to overcome the realities of change.

I remember talking with a wise friend years ago about the process of identity change, and how the major shifts in my life have felt so natural—and yet I have found myself worrying that people would think I was pretending, either for the last decade or in the present moment.

"You're looking at it the wrong way. It's not about pretending. Maybe you're just finally *allowing* yourself to be the person you were supposed to be from the beginning," he said, channeling Paulo Coelho.

Change is worth it, love, and so are you. Learning how to anticipate, weigh, and mitigate the ripple effects of your decisions will save you years of grief by ensuring that you spend more time evaluating decisions *strategically* before changes are implemented rather than cleaning up messes *emotionally* after the fact. What's more, going into a situation with clear eyes and a resolute heart will give you the extra confidence and stability needed to make your change really stick.

Closing Exercise: *If/Then/And*

As you contemplate the changes your bold choice will necessitate, I invite you to run as many scenarios as you can through the "If/When/And" matrix on page 121. What doors will open as a result of this decision? What doors might slam shut? How long will it realistically take to get where you want to go? What will you be asked to sacrifice along the way? What kind of impact will there be on your mental, emotional, and spiritual well-being? Please be thorough and specific as you anticipate the consequences of your decision.

	If . . .	Then . . .	And
Finances			
Time and Energy			
Relationships and Family Dynamics			
Personal Development			

Part III

Time for Action

8

The Playbook

Inaction breeds doubt and fear. Action breeds confidence and courage. If you want to conquer fear, do not sit home and think about it. Go out and get busy.
   —Dale Carnegie

I n the opening chapters, we dug into *why* you want to make a change in your life. Then we explored *what* you want that change to look like. Now, let's discuss *how*, specifically, you will implement that change. That is the boiled-down process of becoming unstuck in three words: *why, what, how.*

How is a critical gap in your journey. My research revealed that nearly 80 percent of respondents said the circumstances that make them feel stuck were changeable, that their problems were solvable. The issue? Only about 30 percent said they had a sense of what *specific steps* are required to achieve the vision they have for their lives.

That's the *how*, and you understand it by mapping out a plan for action.

Whatever your "it" is—that thing you want to change or do,

redefine or repattern, shift or, finally, stop—it's not enough to simply put the longing out into the Universe and hope for the best. It's not enough to think about it obsessively or flog yourself because you haven't yet accomplished it. (If it were, nine years wouldn't have elapsed from the time I first vocalized my intention to write this book and the moment it was released into the world.)

Talk is just that: talk. And if it's not backed by action, talk isn't only cheap; it is the emptiest currency.

"Everyone who has ever taken a shower has had an idea," said Nolan Bushnell, the video game pioneer who founded Atari and, later, Chuck E. Cheese entertainment restaurants. "It's the person who gets out of the shower, dries off, and does something about it that makes a difference."[1]

But before you go running off, half-cocked, compelled to do something, *anything*, in the name of change, you must lay down a plan that is forward-thinking, strategic, resolute. Don't confuse nervous energy with right energy. Otherwise, you risk the kinds of serious missteps that come from not knowing where you're going: starting off in the wrong direction, getting completely lost, finding yourself paralyzed amid disorientation and fear.

I refer to this part of our work as "making the playbook."

The nomenclature isn't mandatory; in fact, you might resonate more with the idea of a roadmap or a blueprint, an easy-to-follow recipe, or the step-by-step instructions that IKEA slides into the box of a chair awaiting assembly. What's more important than the metaphor is what you commit to doing.

But remember: a plan is only as solid as its execution. You can voice your intent to make dinner. You can go to the grocery store, buy all the necessary ingredients, even get out the fancy dishes and silverware—but unless you actually *make* the meal, there will be no food on the table. And you will still be hungry.

Intention without action is just wishful thinking.

Different kinds of situations call for different kinds of playbooks. If the change you seek is relatively straightforward, such as learning a new skill to switch professions, your plan can be straightforward, too. If you need to navigate yourself out of a sticky situation, your plan will require more savvy, nuance, and emphasis on trade-offs, consequences, and boundaries. And if your goal is to, finally, fulfill the big dream of a lifetime, your plan will bring shape and structure and weight to something that previously was an amorphous desire floating out there in the ether.

> **Intention without action is just wishful thinking.**

Whether your goal calls for a discrete, one-off change or a complete life overhaul, the plan you develop will help answer one of my favorite old questions: *How do you eat an elephant? Same way you eat anything else: one bite at a time.*

There is no workable plan that moves a person from point A to point Q in a single, uninterrupted, unobstructed leap. A smart playbook will draw a line first from point A to point B . . . then B to C . . . C to D . . . and so on—little bites of the elephant. There is no way to circumvent the hard work that must be done. There are no shortcuts. But a string of small, standalone actions can ladder up, over time, to something truly meaningful. You win when you execute the plan you've laid out.

Every good playbook will include at least these three elements:

- Specific actions that support your long-term goal;
- Realistic timelines for getting them done; and
- Relevant yardsticks, whether quantitative or qualitative, to measure progress against your unique definition of success.

A Personalized Approach

Despite overlap in our individual values, our common fears, and shared core human desires, every person's playbook will look different because the specifics of every situation are different. Family of origin circumstances and life experiences play an enormous role, as do the impacts of racial and gender bias, the state of mental and physical and emotional health, financial security or insecurity, access to education and opportunity, the presence of role models and support networks, and many more factors.

Not one of us has had an experience identical to another's, nor will we; the past, present, and future hold too many variables.

Still, it's helpful to peek inside others' playbooks for insight and inspiration. Here are a few examples.

Michael and The Middle Way

Michael, an executive at a tech firm in California, had reached a stage in his life—mid-forties, married for nearly twenty years, with aging parents, and newly sober—where he felt stuck and craved more balance. He wanted to adopt more of the "Middle Way" approach outlined in Buddhism, which, for him, looked like finding the sweet spot between contentment and always wanting/needing/searching for more.

Michael also sought a greater sense of choice and freedom when it came to deciding what he wanted to do and how he wanted to do it. "For a while, I've felt like I've been racing to do what everyone else needs, searching for external validation and acceptance, both in my work and my personal life," he said. "That has led me to feeling overwhelmed and exhausted because it's never enough, which then leads me to self-destructive behaviors like numbing or checking out. I'm looking to derive my value from the inside out."

For his first playbook, Michael turned his attention to quality versus quantity at the office. "A more manageable workload means I can better focus on the work I take on—and feel good not just about the outcomes, but the work itself." Step one was to talk with his boss about reducing the scope of his job responsibilities. He then laid down a detailed plan outlining next actions: list out specific responsibilities and tasks he wanted to transition and to whom; propose and agree on a timeline for offloading the work; create a thorough transition plan with a timeline for moving assignments to their new owners; draft a new job description with reduced scope of responsibilities; communicate the news to colleagues who would be impacted by the change; brief the new owners on everything they needed to know to be successful; and then focus, focus, focus on doing the best job he could with the work he retained.

The act of putting the plan down on paper was an immense help, Michael said. "I tend to avoid taking initial steps in a project because I think I have to have it all figured out and 'done in my head' before I start something. Seeing it in steps helped me realize that I had more of it figured out than I thought. And it helped me hold myself accountable as I gave myself permission to take it just one step at a time."

Mary's Desire for a Simple, Full Life

Mary is a mom of three kids in elementary school who was overwhelmed and stuck, not by parenting, but by the "stuff" that comes with it.

Standing on the core values of time, kindness, patience, wisdom, and presence, the focus of Mary's playbook was an area she called "the most obvious, easiest place to start," but also one that felt impossible: *simplify*. "When I was sitting in your class dreaming about the life I long for, I kept imagining myself in my home without the stress and distraction of a cluttered house," she told me. "I realized I've been on autopilot wrapped up in a 'busy, full life' while daydreaming about a 'simple, full life.' But I can feel a difference in my body and my soul when my physical space is clean, decluttered, and comforting—so no more daydreaming! Let's simplify!"

Mary's motivation to simplify was to have more opportunity to care for herself and her family. "Less 'stuff' means less time spent putting crap away and more time spent having fun with my favorite people in the world," she said. "Less 'stuff' means less money wasted on shit we don't need. Less 'stuff' means less time spent working to pay for all the stuff I don't need so I can spend that time enjoying life instead." Not all her reasons were so practical, though. "I grew up in a home that was physically and emotionally cluttered, and I don't want to pass that on to the next generation."

When Mary shared the first action of her simplification playbook—returning a giant stack of overdue books to the library—she earned big smiles and a round of applause from the rest of the group. Could there have been a more perfect first step? The next items on her list were to re-engage with an online community dedicated to minimalism; to re-read a favorite book on the topic; and to have what she called a Monday Morning Meeting with Myself, in which she would review goals and priorities for the week, identify anything that could be let go, and then schedule time blocks for activities such as purging, dropping off donations and returns, grocery shopping, going for a hike, reading, practicing yoga, and dedicating time for rest.

Committing these and other actions to the playbook was essential for building momentum, Mary said. "I'm really good at overthinking and overwhelming myself, and not so good at just doing something. The playbook gave me a place to start and a level of accountability. As an Obliger (Gretchen Rubin's *The Four Tendencies*[2]), I need external accountability. Even though this playbook was created by me, I still feel like it's an external demand because it's not in my head, it's actually on paper. And everything is doable! These aren't big lofty goals like 'my house must be clean at all times' or 'my garage must be empty by an arbitrary date.' These are small steps to get me going on a long journey."

Erin Unties the Knot

Many years ago, I worked with a young woman I'll call Erin. She had gotten married against her own better judgment at age twenty-five and, just a few months into it, knew she needed to get out. She felt like a failure, guilty for having put family and friends through the effort and expense of a wedding only to recognize so early she'd made a dreadful mistake.

Worse, though, was her husband's temperament: he had been acting violently toward her and she feared there would be a physical altercation if she told him she wanted to leave. Erin was crystal clear on the decision to end the marriage, but unsure how to do it without a major confrontation.

No one else was aware just how seriously their relationship had deteriorated, so she didn't know to whom to turn for help. We sat down together to sketch out a series of strategic actions designed to get her out of the house safely. Altogether, her plan contained fewer than fifty words: (1) Tell my parents, (2) Secure bank account and get cash in hand, (3) Retain an attorney, (4) Ask the police what kind of help is available, (5) Arrange for a safe, undisclosed place to stay, (6) Get boxes, (7) Pack while he's at work, (8) Take what I need and leave.

One element each of these playbooks has in common is what I call "think/say/do alignment." As Gandhi put it, "Happiness is when what you think, what you say, and what you do are in harmony." The opposite—when you are out of alignment—is when you think one thing but say another, or make a promise to yourself or others but don't follow through, or your actions are incongruent with your values.

Think of your playbook, then, as your integrity in written form—and your execution of it an act of honoring that integrity.

Think of your playbook, then, as your integrity in written form—and your execution of it an act of honoring that integrity.

Creating New Habits

The most tangible way to honor your plan, your new direction, is to reinforce the habits that support it. In his book *Atomic Habits,* James Clear makes the case succinctly:

> *Your outcomes are a lagging measure of your habits. Your net worth is a lagging measure of your financial habits. Your weight is a lagging measure of your eating habits. Your knowledge is a lagging measure of your learning habits. Your clutter is a lagging measure of your cleaning habits. You get what you repeat.*[3]

Before I embraced sobriety, for example, my inability to take the direction of my life into my own two hands was a lagging measure of my drinking habits. It was that deep avoidance of an uncomfortable reality, as well as the reluctance to be honest with myself about what I felt and what I needed, that landed me deeper and deeper into the quicksand of Other People's Expectations—not to mention the fuzzy, horizonless anguish of a twenty-year hangover. By habitually escaping from my life, I had relinquished any sense of agency to guide it. I got what I repeated.

But when I quit drinking, I was forced to lose old behaviors and create new ones that would reinforce my freedom rather than quash it.

My new life became a measure of my choosing habits: every time I reached for a cup of tea instead of a glass of wine, every time I chose to stay in an uncomfortable moment rather than numb it, every time I chose to live by design rather than be carried on a wave of past momentum, every time I chose honesty over meekness or convenience, I became more *me*. Over time, each positive choice in support of my Self paved the way for another, and another, until I was riding the waves of the momentum I created.

Again, from James Clear: "Every action you take is a vote for the type of person you wish to become. The most practical way to change *who* you are is to change *what* you do."[4] And, from the writer Victoria Erickson: "If you inherently long for something, become it first. If you want gardens, become the gardener."[5]

What new habits will you need to form to support your broader goal? What old ones will you need to break and replace with better ones? Building in the time and opportunity for your new habits to become ingrained—not just in your schedule but in your character—is essential to your think/say/do alignment.

Motivation and Regret

If we know one thing, one thing at all, it's that change is not easy. If it was, if it was frictionless and rapturous and came with no threat of backlash, then we would *never* feel stuck. Instead, we'd glide from situation to situation, mixing things up every time they felt uncomfortable.

No, meaningful change can be excruciating, maddening, even regrettable at times. Because true metamorphosis alters far more than the circumstances around you; it dissolves your old patterns from the inside out. As my friends in Alcoholics Anonymous say: "We thought we could find an easier, softer way. But we could not."[6] That's why sticking close to your motivation as you upend major parts of your existence is so critical.

Motivation does not come from a fixed perspective; like your values, what compels you to action will evolve over time, in relationship both to your immediate needs and desires as well as your long-term goals.

When I first quit drinking, my motivation was urgent and read more like a desperate prayer than the soft current of long-game inspiration: *God, I beg you, exorcise this demon from my body and my mind. Just for this moment, make this craving disappear.*

As the days advanced, the ground beneath me began to solidify and I could feel the stability and strength of that came from standing on my own two legs as opposed to

> No longer moved by a desire to flee a life I didn't want, I became free to pursue the one I did.

the hollow, staggering stilts of the previous two decades. What compelled me to keep going was a new sensation: clearheaded certainty over what I needed from this life experience, done wishing my days away, finally able to breathe with a sense of

Self-respect. No longer moved by a desire to flee a life I didn't want, I became free to pursue the one I did—the one I still do.

Still, the threat of regret can linger even if the "why" behind it has shifted, because motivation and regret are two sides of the same coin: *I have chosen to _____ because I want to feel _____, but if I fail to keep this promise to my Self, I will experience _____.*

While the notion of regret has undertones of roads not taken and ships that sailed or fuckups unmitigated, leaving you to choke in the dust of either bad or unmade choices, it is not an entirely useless emotion. Regret points to a south star, that thing you don't want. As my longings for alcohol gave way to craving instead the feelings of expansiveness and peace sobriety so kindly offered, regret would sidle up to me, slyly opening his jacket to reveal the shame, disappointment, and self-loathing that could be all mine if I would just break the promise I had made. But I was firm. *No way, buddy. Get lost. I'm keeping this sweetness.*

As you commit your action plan to paper, pause and ask: What regrets would you have if you didn't follow through? How would you feel? What would you lose? You can use that insight to fuel your progress and keep your motivation strong.

Accountability

A good friend of motivation—and the antidote to regret—is accountability.

Accountability means taking full ownership of our choices, our words, our actions and inactions. It means being answerable for them. And while life may make us *responsible* for a great deal, such as performing the job functions for which we get paid or living up to promises made in relationships, ultimately, we are *answerable* only to ourselves. The karma of natural consequences—employer cans you, partner decides to walk away—takes care of the rest.

Yet it is difficult to be accountable in a vacuum, because promises made in secret are quite difficult to keep.

Think back to the times in your life when you made a notable commitment. Did you do so publicly or privately?

> Yet it is difficult to be accountable in a vacuum, because promises made in secret are quite difficult to keep.

Most things meaningful are announced in some way, often as a signal for celebration but also as a sign of accountability: we pledge a sorority, we confirm commitment to a religious group, we take a seat on a board, we marry. (Fascinating statistic: A 2014 survey of people who had ever married showed that couples who had as few as ten people witness their wedding were 35 percent less likely to divorce than those who had eloped. Those who had two hundred guests were 92 percent less likely to divorce.[7]) Accountability, it seems, matters.

That's because we need to be witnessed.

We need encouragement and support to keep us going when it would feel easier to just stop.

And, very often, we need more than the ol' *atta girl!*; we need specific, tangible help.

As a woman with a hot streak of codependency running through me—in particular, an overdeveloped sense of responsibility—I used to find it quite challenging to ask for any kind of assistance, embodying the notion that if you want something done right, do it yourself. There was also that societal pressure born from liberation run amok—the idea of the modern woman as someone who could have it all—that raised the bar too high for an entire generation. Foolishly, I thought that meant I had to *do* it all; worse, I thought I *could*. Talk about an indigestion of shoulds! With the realization that I *could not*—nor, to be honest, did I *want to*—I forced myself to get more comfortable with asking for, and receiving, help.

Asking for Help

The musician Amanda Palmer is a crowdfunding pioneer who has elevated asking into a serious art form. First she raised $1.2 million from her fans in 2012 to fund the creation of an album, book, and music tour. A few years later she joined the service Patreon, through which thousands of fans pay a buck (or more) per download to provide what she calls "ongoing, reliable support—akin to a salary 'in the real world.'"

In her 2014 book *The Art of Asking*, Palmer likened every one of her creative offerings, for which she asks for money in return, as a bid at connection, an act of trust:

> *We make countless choices every day whether to ask or to turn away from one another. Wondering whether it's too much to ask the neighbor to feed the cat. The decision to turn away from a partner, to turn off the light instead of asking what's wrong. Asking for help requires authenticity, and vulnera-*

bility. Those who ask without fear learn to say two things, with or without words, to those they are facing: I deserve to ask and You are welcome to say no.[8]

Do you believe that? That you deserve to ask and others are welcome to say no?

If you do, you're a step ahead. If not, may I suggest that you try the concept on for size, introducing it slowly with that framework as your foundation, and see how it feels? You might be surprised at what a relief it is to ask for help when you need it . . . and to say no when you need that, too. The right to seek help, and the choice to provide it or not, is equal for both asker and askee. (Beloved chronic people pleasers, I'm lookin' at you here.)

It's Playbook Time

At this point, I'm going to ask you to stop reading and start making your playbook. You can lay it out in the form of a to-do list, a collage, a diagram, a timeline, a vision board, a bound book. Frame it on a whiteboard or a chalk wall. Create the world's most tricked-out PowerPoint presentation if that will give you the extra kick in the pants you need to stay motivated and on track.

Please take as much time to create your playbook as you need. Allow it to marinate for a spell and then come back to add detail and deadlines. Decorate it, color it, laminate it, whatever makes it real.

If you let your dream be just a thought in your head, it's possible that's all it will ever be. But if you stake out a clear path

> If you let your dream be just a thought in your head, it's possible that's all it will ever be.

forward, in a format that resonates with you, then all that's left is the execution. And I believe that if you've gotten *this* far, you're gonna execute like a motherfucker.

Closing Exercise: *Making the Playbook*

Referring back to all the insights you gained from previous exercises for direction, it's time to create your playbook (or map or recipe or instruction manual, whatever metaphor resonates best). What are the next actions, near-term and long-term, you need to take to address your "not this" and support your values, priorities, *your soul-guided choices*?

As you envision the life you want, what do you need to learn, do, defer, adjust, or eliminate to get first from point A to point B . . . and then eventually to points D, J, Q, or wherever your ultimate destination lies? How will you prioritize your next steps? How will you communicate them to others and stay accountable to your Self? Whom will you ask for help? Factor in the trade-offs, consequences, and boundaries identified in the previous chapter's closing exercise and consider angles such as: *Where will I invest the bulk of my energy and time? What am I willing to sacrifice? Where might I need to reevaluate?*

9

Care for the Journey

I kneel in front of a new altar
  in honor of my heart, emotions,
  and my mamas and her mamas.
  In that place I lay down,
  and I don't sleep.
  I awaken.
  —Octavia Raheem

The moment you take the first step in your playbook, you are pushing off from one shore and it will be some time before your feet land on another. This is "liminal space," what author Nancy Levin beautifully coined "the space between no longer and not yet"[1]; what one of my unofficial mentors, Heather Plett, likened to the breathtaking moment "when a trapeze artist lets go of one bar and doesn't yet know whether they will be able to catch the other."[2]

It is worth pausing here to honor where you have been, where you are going, and where you are in this moment. To throw off the heavy chains of your past and decide to live your life in a bold and perhaps unfamiliar way demands an incredible amount of courage. It takes more trust in your Self and in the Universe than you may ever have thought possible.

Know that what you are doing is spectacular and audacious, in the very best way. Your bravery will not go unnoticed; in fact, your actions are radiant and propagating. You are divine, inspired, and finally stepping into the future that is distinctly yours. And for anyone who might question your ability and your grit—well, honey, they can go eat a bag of hockey pucks.

Liminal Space

I first heard the phrase "liminal space" back in 2014 when a friend told me I was in the thick of it, and the situation demanded that I treat my Self with "exquisite tenderness." She was right to tell me that, and now I want to tell *you*. If you love your Self enough to make this bold change in your life, you damn well better love your Self enough to do it right. Navigating this uncertain and sometimes terrifying white space between what you have known and what you long for requires great care.

But what does that tenderness entail? What does it look like to support your Self in times of upheaval and growth? How can you stand tall when the ground under your feet feels so unsteady?

Self-care was already a buzz phrase of the twenty-first century before the COVID-19 pandemic elevated concerns over mental wellness and revealed what a terrible job most of us do to care for ourselves in challenging times. By and large, we minimize our needs, deprioritize them below others', or ignore them altogether rather than tend directly to them. We neglect when we should nurse, avoid when we should attend.

In her outstanding book *The Art of Holding Space,* Plett described it this way: "Your goal in holding space for yourself is to keep your psychic membrane healthy and strong so that it can protect and nourish you. When it is tired, overworked, or undervalued, it doesn't function well, and you are left unprotected and undernourished."[3]

To move closer to the life you dream of you will need a nourished, cared-for body; a sharp, determined, and unburdened mind; and an uncaged soul that is free and empowered to lead the way. You will need to be in tune with all the elements of your being, speaking their language, so you know when to push and when to rest. Self-care, Self-nourishment, Self-healing, Self-love—all of this is the work of your lifetime. It's what makes the rest of this (gestures broadly) possible and, dare I say, *enjoyable.*

This journey must not be a trudge, a relentless death march, or you risk losing not just your motivation but your very ability to move forward. Remember, the journey itself is a sign of commitment to your deepest Self, a raised banner shouting your liberation, a celebration of your very soul, a healing of your past and your future both.

Treat personal growth like a miserable grind and it will feel that way; treat it like power and joy and watch what happens. This is your freedom unfolding.

Your Prescription

During the height of the COVID-19 pandemic, when the bulk of my work was done virtually, I had a student who hilariously noted our Zoom appointments on her calendar as "telehealth appointment with Dr. Vollmer" so that no one would schedule a conflicting meeting during that time. I'm no doctor, of course, but if I could write you a prescription for sustaining your integrity during this journey, it would look something like this:

"Regular purification and fortification of body, mind, and spirit for energy, clarity, and peace. Chocolate chip cookies as needed. Doctor's orders."

If you think of your playbook as your integrity on paper, you can think of caring for your Self in a holistic way during this liminal time as the way you feed and honor your soul's integrity.

In the pages that follow, I want to share the practices that have most helped me evolve, find comfort, and stay sane over the years. (Okay, *relatively* sane.) This is not an exhaustive summary, but it does reach across the planes of physical body, thinking brain, and connection with Self and Source to encompass the entirety of the human experience.

Experts tout the value of ritual and routine when it comes to incorporating these practices. And while I don't doubt the validity of that approach, I'll be honest and tell you I've never quite gotten into the habit of something like a morning ritual. I like my routine "baggy enough to live in," as the writer Matt Haig describes it,[4] so I approach Self-care in more of a buffet style, working in at least three of these elements at some point in a day, mixing and matching as the mood strikes.

Sometimes that looks like twenty minutes of morning journaling with a candle burning in my line of sight followed by an evening bath to wind down; other days it's an hour on my yoga mat during which I move, breathe, and sit quietly for meditation; other days it's curling up with a soft kitty and a warm blanket for an afternoon snooze on the couch. (Or is it a warm kitty and a soft blanket? I've got both.) What's important is that we make the time for our own nurturing and growth in a time of uncertainty and change.

Here are seven essential practices to make life easier during your liminal journey, and beyond. The point of all this is not to overwhelm you with more to do. On the contrary, I believe you'll find these actions to be restorative and generative. They will not deplete you, but instead fill you up, enliven you, balance you, make you more whole and more fully *you*.

1. Movement and breath
2. Mindfulness and meditation
3. Letting go

4. Cultivating emotional intelligence
5. Therapy
6. Journaling
7. Comfort and rest

Movement and Breath

In Chapter 5, we discussed the physical benefit of yoga, specifically how it helps to activate the body's parasympathetic nervous system and move us out of "fight, flight, or freeze" stress response.

We often talk about what stimulates that response in terms that our caveman ancestors would appreciate, like the old example of being chased by a tiger. But here in twenty-first-century America, most of us aren't getting chased by tigers—or anything else, for that matter. Instead, the stressors we encounter are often *chronic* (think work, parenting, relationships, etc.) and *emotional* (anger, frustration, injustice, overwhelm). Even if we find ways to calm down emotionally, that physical stress remains in the body, just waiting—and needing—to be discharged.

"Dealing with your *stress* is a separate process from dealing with the things that cause your stress. To deal with your *stress*, you have to *complete the cycle* . . . Physical activity is the single most efficient strategy for completing the stress response cycle," sisters Emily and Amelia Nagoski write in *Burnout: The Secret to Unlocking the Stress Cycle*.[5]

This means, in simplest terms, you need to move. Burn. Purify. Run, jump, wiggle, shake, skate, swim, dance, box, burpee, lift, walk, whatever—just move!

What I love most about the physical aspect of yoga—which is my chosen form of movement, and so much more—is that it's a whole-body experience.

By working all the major joints and muscle groups, the practice promotes mobility, stability, strength, and balance. I can dial the intensity up or down as I wish. Yoga has taught me how to discern between approaching my edge and passing unsafely beyond my limits, how to stay mindfully in discomfort rather than fleeing the moment things get tough.

Beyond that, yoga is something I can do by myself and with my Self; it requires no competitor, no team, no special shoes or clothes or machinery. The practice is adaptable for times when I'm tired or dealing with injury or in the parts of my menstrual cycle when all I want to do is lay belly-down on my bolster in child's pose; it's portable, which means I can do it literally anywhere (supine poses in the park, standing poses in my living room, seated movements at my desk or even in an airplane); and, once you get familiar with the basic principles and shapes, it's free. No-cost stress reduction!

As I mature, I find that what I like even better than yoga *asana* ("postures" in Sanskrit) is breathwork (*pranayama*).

As we touched on earlier, deep and slow breathing stimulates the vagus nerve, helping the body trade the stress hormones for the more relaxing ones. Beyond calming, there are also breathing techniques designed to expand lung function, energize the body, balance the right and left sides of the brain, reduce anxiety, and promote sleep.

Different yoga lineages have their own preferred styles—you may have heard of other techniques such as belly breathing, box breathing, sun breath, lion's breath, breath of fire, alternate nostril breathing, etc. (If you are curious to learn more about yogic breathwork, the book *Light on Pranayama* by B. K. S. Iyengar is considered the benchmark. He goes into great detail on advanced techniques that involve things like changing the ratio of inhale to exhale, retaining the breath, chopping it up into smaller pieces, forcing it out at a rapid rate, and more.)

Of course, one doesn't need to be a yogi to work with the breath; beyond the ancient yogic practice of *pranayama*, there are other, newer modalities of breathing techniques you might explore. But the fundamental yogic methods of controlling breath and energy have survived over thousands of years because they are so simple and effective. Even Navy SEALs recommend it![6] And, like yoga movement, breathing is accessible, adaptable, portable, and completely free.

> It is far more valuable to have a simple, consistent practice than an advanced but inconsistent one.

While I have indeed found benefit to some of the more complex practices, I can tell you this: *It is far more valuable to have a simple, consistent practice than an advanced but inconsistent one.* As my old boss used to remind us in the PR biz, the key to success is *consistency and persistency, over time.* This applies to life outside of yoga as well.

Yoga practice, whether focused on physical poses or breathwork, need not be fancy or expert-level to be richly effective and life-changing. The objective of any breath practice, regardless of lineage or technique, is to interact less with thoughts and senses in order to transcend the mind and connect with the soul.

Shorthand: *Quiet the mind*.

Every time you become distracted by thought—and you *will* become distracted by thought—just return to noticing the rhythm of your breath and refocus. It is literally that simple—and what makes this a practice.

Here are three of my favorite beginner techniques if you'd like to give them a try. Begin each by finding a comfortable seat in a chair or on the floor.

- *Sama vrtti pranayama* (Sanskrit for "equal length breathing"): The goal of this practice is to even out the length of the inhale and the exhale. Begin by closing the eyes (or, if that feels uncomfortable, relaxing the gaze) and simply noticing the breath. Notice if one part, either the inhale or the exhale, seems to be longer. Over the course of several rounds of breath, even out the length of inhale and exhale. You may find it useful to count in your head to bring inhale and exhale to the same length. Then, begin to slow the breath so that inhales and exhales become longer, and still equal. If you begin, say, with a count of 3 or 4 or 5, try to lengthen to a 4 or 5 or 6. (A count of 5 in and 5 out makes for a count of 10 for a full cycle of breath, or 6 breaths per minute.) Continue deepening for five to ten minutes, then return to normal breathing. Over time, and with practice, you may slow your breath to 3 or 4 breaths per minute and practice for a longer period, say, twenty minutes. This is wonderful breath to practice lying on your mat, sitting at your desk, or waiting in the carpool pickup lane at your child's school.

- *Ujjayi pranayama* ("victorious breath"): This technique builds on the equal breathing outlined above by adding sound, sometimes likened to ocean waves or "Darth Vader" breath. We make this sound by activating the muscles at the back of the throat. Try this to see what I mean: Exhale the slow "ha" sound you might make if you were fogging up your glasses to clean them. Now, make it more gently. Now make the same sound with the mouth closed, drawing in your inhale and letting out your exhale with the throat muscles slightly activated. That is the basic sound of *ujjayi* breath.

  To practice *ujjayi*, you'll begin with the long, slow inhales and exhales of *sama vrtti pranayama* described above, and then gently introduce the ocean wave sound. Do this slowly, like you would gradually turn up the volume on music rather than just flipping a switch to full blast. The sound of *ujjayi* is easy, not forced, and relatively quiet. (It would be audible to a person sitting next to you, perhaps, but not someone across the room.) Remember to keep the muscles of the face, jaw, and eyes soft as you focus on the breath rather than the thoughts of the mind. Practice for five or ten minutes, either seated or lying down, before returning to natural breath. *Ujjayi* breath also can be practiced while flowing through yoga postures (vinyasa yoga).

- *Bhramari pranayama* ("bee breath"): This breath technique also incorporates sound, but in a much different way. With *bhramari*, you make an audible "mmmmm" sound, mimicking a bumblebee, on the exhale breath. Begin in a seated position, closing the eyes and deepening the breath, in and out through the nose. Draw in a deep, full inhale and, on the exhale, make the humming sound with mouth closed until all the breath is gone. Repeat a deep, full inhale followed by the long, audible "mmmmm" exhale. Completely empty your breath to facilitate the next deep inhale and repeat. In humming bee breath, your exhale will be significantly longer than the inhale. During *bhramari* breath, you can close off the ears to deepen the sensation within, using your fingers to press down on the tragus (the thick bit of cartilage that partially covers the ear canal). You can also use your thumbs to press down on the tragus while your fingers cover the eyes.

(A note of caution: If you at any time become dizzy, lightheaded, or develop a headache while practicing pranayama, please stop and return to your normal breath.)

Mindfulness and Meditation

Beyond focusing on the breath, yoga guides us to practice mindfulness by concentrating attention on something specific such as a *mantra* (a silently repeated sound, syllable, or phrase) or a candle flame. A Christian tradition of meditation, called Centering Prayer, guides practitioners to come back to a sacred word of their choosing.

The Buddhist tradition of mindfulness is somewhat different, encouraging us to notice the various thoughts, sensations, and emotions that arise when we are still, meeting them with curiosity and compassion. This kind of mindfulness you can practice anytime, anyplace: as water from the shower falls on your head; as you slowly eat a meal and notice the consistency, temperature, flavor of each bite of food; as you face the sun and feel the sensation of warmth and wind on your skin; as you walk a labyrinth or even in your backyard, placing each footstep quietly and carefully upon the earth; as you sit in a forward bend and notice, without any judgment, the tension in your hamstrings or the pressure of your inhale against your back ribs; as an uncomfortable emotion arises and you meet it with curiosity rather than frustration.

This practice of noticing—without wishing that you, or your thoughts, or anything else that arises in the moment were different and instead simply acknowledging what is—is simple, yet far from easy. Especially in the beginning. That's because we have mistaken the act of "observation" for "judgment," and, innate to that confusion are the pernicious ideas of expectation and comparison. ("Expectation is the root of all heartache" and "Comparison is the thief of joy," as commonly attributed, or misattributed, to Shakespeare and Teddy Roosevelt, respectively.)

My teacher Pam explains the confluence of observation, judgment, expectation, and comparison in a language I can really sink my teeth into: pizza.

Imagine you're meeting friends at a restaurant the top local magazine has rated "the best pizza in town" (expectation). The server arrives and sets down the pie. You all tear into it and here come the comments: "This crust is too chewy." "The cheese is awfully stringy." "Whoa, way too much sauce!" The group proclamation is "meh" (judgment) and there's a collective sense of letdown because the pizza doesn't live up to the hype (disappointment). "The pizza I had last week was way better than this!" you say (comparison). You leave disappointed and the anticipated joy doesn't materialize.

Now imagine that you come to the experience never having eaten pizza or seen reviews of this particular restaurant. You don't go in with any expectations or a baseline for comparison. When the pizza arrives, you observe rather than judge; the sauce, for example, isn't *too much* sauce or *too little* sauce. It isn't *good* sauce or *bad* sauce. *It's just sauce.* There is no disappointment, just a meal.

At some point you may *discern* that you don't, in fact, *like* pizza . . . and *decide that you'd rather have something else instead.* Perfectly fine; that choice is yours to make. That discernment, however, is entirely separate from the mindfulness practice that can introduce you to meditation. In mindfulness, we simply observe and allow.

Paying attention is the doorway from mind to spirit. Presence is the threshold. And mindfulness that leads to meditation is the room we seek to enter.

> Paying attention is the doorway from mind to spirit. Presence is the threshold. And mindfulness that leads to meditation is the room we seek to enter.

People often ask me what meditation feels like, and when I answer, I feel like words are tragically inadequate. How does one describe seeing the vast magnificence of the Grand Canyon for the first time? Or the most epic orgasm ever had? Or the volume of emotion a heart in love can hold before it bursts? It's like all of this combined, multiplied by a gazillion, with a dollop of cosmic hot fudge on top.

In transcending mindfulness and moving into a state of meditation, I am enveloped in a sacred, infinite tranquility. There is often an experience of lost time. As I sit with palms on thighs, I've had the sensation of the body melting into itself; the hands and legs are no longer separate entities but dissolve to become part of each other. Breathing can slow to a near standstill and there is the glorious feeling in the soul of being infused with and absorbed by the light, energy, and consciousness of Source. *Sweet, divine union.*

These feelings don't occur all at once or every time I sit; truth is this sensation can be quite elusive, especially in the beginning. And, even after practicing for nearly twenty years, I can still become frustrated with my chitty-chatty monkey mind and find my ego tempted to walk away in annoyance. But that is when I come back. That is *why* I come back, again and again and again, to quiet the loquaciousness of the ego and hear instead the wisdom of my inner being.

> "In an age of speed, I began to think nothing could be more invigorating than going slow. In an age of distraction, nothing can feel more luxurious than paying attention. And in an age of constant movement, nothing is more urgent than sitting still." —Pico Iyer

Pico Iyer, in his book *The Art of Stillness: Adventures in Going Nowhere,* said it this way: "In an age of speed, I began to think nothing could be more invigorating than going slow. In an age of distraction, nothing can feel more luxurious than paying attention. And in an age of constant movement, nothing is more urgent than sitting still."[7]

Letting Go

In the moments when I struggle to make sense of life, I take my yoga off the mat, calling upon many of the ancient teachings and philosophies that transcend time. Here are just four: *impermanence, non-attachment, acceptance,* and *contentment*.

These concepts guide my thoughts and actions, bring me deep comfort, and feel as relevant today in our fast-paced, tech-driven, global society as they would have two thousand years ago.

While each one is a distinct notion, they do build onto one another—and, taken together, allow for a great letting go.

Impermanence

Everything ends, all of it. The body that was born, the thoughts that come and go, emotional states, relationships, creatures and plants of nature. Every life, every circumstance, every feeling, every material possession, every bit of existence is fleeting and temporary; it comes into being and then dissolves. What remains is your divinity, your soul, your Self.

In yoga philosophy, this state of human impermanence (in contrast to the permanence of the Soul) is called *asthira* in Sanskrit. Slightly different is the idea that the only constant is change. As the Greek philosopher Heraclitus put it: "A man never steps in the same river twice, for it's not the same river and he's not the same man." That mindset, called *parinamavada*, reminds us we live in a state of flux, not stone. How freeing!

When we understand that our stories are written in pencil rather than ink, we are relieved of the crushing pressure of *forever*. (Ironically, it was my belief in impermanence that convinced me, at age forty, to finally begin getting the tattoos I'd wanted all my life.) Because of impermanence, mistakes can fade into memories and lessons rather than stand as looming memorials to poor judgment. We can become less interested in sweating the proverbial "small stuff" and more inclined to go bold on the big stuff. And we begin to see so much of life is small stuff; all that burns, all that angers, all that cuts you up at the knees is transitory. Tomorrow will be different, even if it takes years to see it.

"Impermanence can teach you a lot about how to cheer up,"[8] Pema Chödrön wrote. "When you open yourself to the continually changing, impermanent, dynamic nature of your own being and of reality, you increase your capacity to love and care about other people and your capacity to not be afraid."[9]

So I'll say it again but this time with a tweak: You are a *temporary* meat-coated skeleton made of stardust; what do you have to be scared of?

Non-Attachment

I hold tightly to the idea of impermanence—but *not too tightly!*—because: non-attachment.

When we are too attached to elements of this human life—the people we love, for instance, or outcomes and effects, emotional or physical sensations, material objects, etc.—we are ripe to suffer.

With attachments come expectations and the instincts to manage. Same goes for aversions.

Foolishly, we believe that anything we either hold tight in our fist or repel like a force field is something we can control. What we don't often see until it is too late is that our attachments and aversions are actually *controlling us*. Everything we covet and avoid, the outcomes we desire, the sensations we crave, all that we fear has the potential to warp our perceptions, blunt our decision-making capabilities, and wreak havoc on our ability to regulate emotions—rendering us, by degrees, subservient and powerless. As the old Zen proverb goes: "Let go or be dragged."

What's more effective than the closed fist of attachment, and more in keeping with the notion of impermanence, is the open-palm energy of *non*-attachment. This is not indifference or a refusal to participate. It is a bow to the ever-changing nature of the world around us and an acknowledgment of the finite realm of human power. *Do we have influence?* Yes. *Agency and choice?* Of course. Yet there are limits. We may extend life but we cannot preclude death, so instead we allow life to happen and seek to maintain equilibrium as it does. This applies to all else we seek to govern.

Return to Heraclitus's thought on the river for a moment: Attachment is rerouting or damming the water so you can exert control over it; aversion is refusing to step in for fear of getting your shoes wet; indifference connotes an apathy toward the river, lack of any interest or regard in the river itself.

Healthy non-attachment, on the other hand, honors the river as it flows unimpeded. You drink freely but don't make a pool to hoard it; you are thankful for the offering but not controlled by it. The river flows and you are at peace. The river dries up and you look for water elsewhere, still at peace.

A prayer in the practice of Centering Prayer, one that is a touchstone for my sobriety, is a lovely blend of mindfulness and non-attachment: *I let go of my desire for security, affection, control, and embrace this moment as it is.* In other words, "If these gifts come, I will appreciate them but I will not be undone by their absence." The goal is not clinging to any external validation, outcome, or material thing. Non-grasping, non-possessing, non-greedy . . . *non-attached.*

Acceptance

"You can't argue with what is," wrote Eckhart Tolle in *A New Earth.* "Well, you can, but if you do, you suffer."[10]

This gets to the heart of acceptance, which follows the letting go of non-attachment.

Acceptance does not mean you lay back and let Life have its way with you. It is not a path of hopeless acquiescence or defeated inaction, nor does it imply that you will ignore hardship or injustice (yours or others'). It simply means that you understand and acknowledge the facts of a given moment. You, as the old saying goes, let reality be reality. And after you accept "it," whatever that is in each moment or situation, you can decide if or how you will respond. (I mean, just because you get served a shit sandwich doesn't mean you have to eat it.)

Let's say, for example, you break your leg a week before you're supposed to run a marathon. Acceptance wouldn't have you sitting at home with your femur snapped in two, untreated;

no, you would go to the doctor, get the bone set in a cast, and do the prescribed physical therapy when the time comes.

Acceptance allows you to take the same matter-of-fact approach to the mental and emotional aspects of a situation, no matter how distasteful. You acknowledge the circumstance for what it is, honor the emotions you feel, and then decide what to do about it. You allow the temporary disturbance to pass over your open palm rather than holding it tightly in your hand, lying on your belly and beating those fists into the ground while hollering about the unfairness of it all. *It is what it is.*

This is easy to grasp when the example is a broken leg. But what about a miserable broken heart? What about a picture of what you thought your life would be that's been shattered into sixty thousand scattered pieces, never to be put together again in any way that makes sense? What about a tragically broken sense of Self?

When you can accept life's pain, challenges, setbacks, complexities, and humiliations as inevitable corollaries to the blessing of the human experience, you suffer less. All the lessons, no matter how long and how many times it takes you to learn them. All the stumbles and trips. All the second chances. All the times you've been too heartsick or too pushed past the mental edge or too afraid or ashamed or simply just didn't give enough of a shit to get out of bed . . . and then something inside you found the courage to do it anyway. "There is something wonderfully bold and liberating about saying yes to our entire imperfect and messy life," therapist and meditation teacher Tara Brach wrote in *Radical Acceptance.*[11]

Of course, the idea of acceptance becomes exponentially more difficult to conceive, much less practice, when the situation is chronic, permanent, represents an unspeakable tragedy or loss, or when an individual truly is powerless. No one expects a person to meet such circumstances with the equanimity of a monk, especially the first time they are encountered. Like anything else, one learns to cope through practice . . . but first, one must accept.

Contentment

It is from this place of acceptance that you can sit in the bliss of contentment (called *santosha* in Sanskrit).

Contentment arises when you stop looking to external sources for validation, pleasure, and peace and instead recognize that you are your own source for happiness; it flows when you understand the transitory nature of every being, material possession, and emotion (positive *and* negative) and can experience both their presence and absence without being knocked over.

Judith Hanson Lasater, the esteemed yoga teacher, described it this way in *Yoga Journal*: "Contentment is not the same as happiness. Contentment is being willing to accept both your happiness and your lack of it at any given moment. Sometimes we are asked to actively remain present with our discontent—to see it as simply what is arising within us, and to look at it with a sense of nonjudgment. This is not a practice for cowards. *Santosha* is a fierce practice that calls upon our dedication and surrender, in each moment of our lives."[12]

When I stand on these four principles—impermanence, nonattachment, acceptance, and contentment—a mantra naturally springs up in me. _Now_, it's like this. And, in the next breath. _Now, it's like this_. Again and again, breath after breath: _Now, it's like this._

From this space of holding loosely to what is temporary and accepting reality, life just flows; no clinging, no aversion, no fighting against what is, no suffering.

When the moment is good, I pause to appreciate before it passes; when the moment is difficult, I recognize it, too, is fleeting and breathe through it. Good, bad, or indifferent: _Now the present situation is like this._ Until it isn't. Either way, I am steady in the changing moment. And in those times when I _do_ become unsteady (because: human), I return to the Serenity Prayer:

> _God, grant me the serenity_
> _to accept the things I cannot change,_
> _courage to change the things I can,_
> _and wisdom to know the difference._

Cultivating Emotional Intelligence

When contentment and serenity feel miles away, it is often because we are Under the Influence of Big Feelings.

Throughout this book I've referenced dozens of different emotions and feelings that crop up in everyday life, from joy and contentment to anger and grief, discomfort, confusion, insecurity, disgust, terror, shame, and more. Your deepest emotions—and the patterns and conditioning ingrained over time that dictate how you express them, or not—have played a tremendous role in the notion that you have been, somehow, stuck.

> Your deepest emotions have played a tremendous role in the notion that you have been, somehow, stuck. If you can understand what your emotions are telling you, and then act on them in productive and meaningful ways, they can play a tremendous role in getting you unstuck, too. But first you must learn to *feel* them.

If you can understand what your emotions are telling you, and then act on them in productive and meaningful ways, they can play a tremendous role in getting you unstuck, too.

But first you must learn to *feel* them.

If "stuck" has been your state of being for any length of time, chances are you unwittingly have a default response to emotions that could include minimizing the triggers that cause them, quashing ones that do arise before they get much of a foothold (aka, Whac-A-Mole), or becoming swept up in a flood of feelings against your will because you haven't yet learned that you can swim among them and not drown. Many trauma survivors and those who did not learn at an early age how to regulate their emotions may experience dissociation, an extreme form of emotional detachment, which renders them emotionally numb to survive the stress of a triggering moment.

But without the ability to understand what important information your emotions are trying to give you, you'll have a very difficult time answering the two fundamental questions I believe every person must be able to answer to move the Self forward:

How do you feel? and *What do you need?*

If the idea of feeling your feelings sounds about as fun as

nagging a teenager to clean up her messy room *yet again,* you're not alone. But good news: Identifying and processing emotions, like any other skill, is learned. And the number of clues your body offers up is remarkable.

Consider the connection of a rapid heart rate to the emotion of anger, how a slow heart rate could indicate depression, or how a jaw that's clenched in irritation feels different from one dropped open in awe. This is why the movement component of yoga—which helps you become aware of, connect with, and build control over your physical body—is so relevant and useful for your emotional development as well.

Remember: *Control the body and you can control the breath; control the breath and you can control the mind.*

Researchers are still debating where and how emotions originate. Some hold there is a small number of basic emotions that are inherently human and universal across cultures; others maintain emotions are multidimensional and influenced largely by culture and individual experience. Those within the "basic emotion" camp differ on what that number is. A therapist told me once there are three: sad, mad, and glad. Some posit four: fear, anger, joy, sadness; others say six, adding to that list surprise and disgust; others believe there are eight, throwing in anticipation and trust.

The topic of identifying, processing, and leveraging emotions and feelings has mushroomed in the zeitgeist of the early twenty-first century. Books like *Emotional Intelligence, The Language of Emotions, Emotional Agility,* and *Permission to Feel* all hold a place of honor on my bookshelf.[13]

Is there a difference between emotions and feelings? Most of us use these terms interchangeably, but you can think of emotions as basic physiological experiences that generate a response in the body (think "fight, flight, freeze, or fawn"), which you may or may not be aware of, and feelings are the conscious, mental associations that rise up out of emotions. Feelings tend to carry more specificity and nuance; for example, awe and dismay are two distinct feelings with entirely different meanings that grow out of the same basic emotion of surprise.

For the purposes of this book, the distinction isn't all that important; just know that emotions and feelings both have the power to shape your outlook on life and your Self, your mood, the quality of your interactions and relationships with others, and your willingness to embrace change and take considered, strategic risks.

If you regularly feel inadequate, insignificant, powerless, or apathetic, chances are you'll be less likely to initiate a big change in, say, your work environment than if you feel curious, inspired, energetic, and respected. If you feel ridiculed by, suspicious of, distant from, and resentful of a person, it's a safe bet you will be hesitant to seek an open, trusting partnership with them.

In our culture, we often think of emotions and feelings as either good (happy!) or bad (angry or sad). Negative ones tend to get more ink and airtime not because they are more prevalent, but because we are less skilled at managing them. It takes significantly more ability and practice to navigate resentment than delight, right? But emotions are not innately negative or in need of being shut down. On the contrary, they are an inherent, essential part of the human experience, one that sets us apart from other animal species.

You can't stop powerful emotions from arising any more

than you can avoid the air you breathe.

> You can't stop powerful emotions from arising any more than you can avoid the air you breathe.

"We truly need our emotions. We can't live functional lives without them. Without our emotions, we can't make decisions; we can't decipher our dreams and visions; we can't set proper boundaries or behave skillfully in relationships; we can't identify our hopes or support the hopes of others; and we can't connect to, or even find, our dearest loves," Karla McLaren wrote in *The Language of Emotions*. "Without access to our emotional selves, we grow in this culture like trees in the wrong soil, becoming tall but not strong, and old but not mature."[14]

Trouble is, too many of us aren't fluent in the language of feelings and therefore lack the vocabulary to identify what is happening inside of us when they arise. It then becomes difficult, if not impossible, to express in a healthy way what we cannot name. And that is a recipe for "stuck," because nothing—*nothing*—will sink your journey to freedom faster than not knowing how to handle Big Feelings when they threaten to knock you off course.

"We've all heard the message: Get over it. Stop focusing on yourself (as though such a thing were possible!). Don't be so sensitive. Time to move on," Marc Brackett writes in *Permission to Feel*. "The irony, though, is that when we ignore our feelings, or suppress them, they only become stronger. The really powerful emotions build up inside us, like a dark force that inevitably poisons everything we do, whether we like it or not. . . . If we don't express our emotions, they pile up like a debt that will eventually come due."[15]

We have to recognize our emotions for what they really

are—not problems to be solved but messengers to be heard. So why haven't more of us been taught *how* to name and feel and express?

In school you probably learned how to multiply fractions, dissect a sentence (and maybe a frog), find Scandinavia on a map, say "Where is the bathroom?" in Spanish or French . . . but no one ever asked you—or, even better, encouraged you to ask yourself—questions like: "How does that make you feel?," "What are you afraid of?," or "Did you know you can calm down by taking deep, slow breaths? Here, let me show you."

Don't blame your parents; no one asked them, either. And *their* parents? *Fuggedaboutit.*

More of this is happening now as children are increasingly taught social awareness skills and self-regulation techniques, thank goodness. But what about those of us in the "Have It All" generation? Where do we go to learn emotional intelligence, fluency, and agility?

The Power of Therapy

Here's where I'll give a deep bow of thanks to social media (in spite of its mega-shortcomings in other areas).

As mental health has leapfrogged to the front of the pack of wellness concerns and our society has become more curious and comfortable talking about emotions, experts have used social media platforms to offer bite-sized-but-powerful nuggets of validation and insight that previously was available only at $150 per session. (If you've ever had an aha moment scrolling memes and carousels, you know precisely what I mean.) Experts and influencers now share more of their personal struggles, previously a no-no but a change that I appreciate immensely. We've learned even therapists have therapists!

And while social media has helped the principles of psychology and psychotherapy go mainstream, when it comes to learning how to notice, process, and leverage your emotions, nothing can compete with the real thing: working one-on-one with a therapist.

The right kind of therapy, with the right therapist, is invaluable. And there's a reason it is the most common first step I see listed in people's playbooks. Take, for example, Selissa.

Selissa, an exhausted mom, had an anger that she was reluctant to admit: Life the last few years with her special-needs son had been hard. She was burned out from rarely getting a break. Even more, she was grieving his diagnosis and a life that was turning out to be much different than the one she had expected. Selissa thought her anger made her a bad person, and she was overwhelmed with guilt because of it. What she hadn't understood, though, was that her anger was a natural part of the grief process.

Selissa's decision to find a therapist to help sort out her emotions was life-changing. Once the therapist showed her that her feelings were normal and valid, the work—and the healing—began. At the center: the concepts of expectations, control, and acceptance, and specific skills to deal with life's constant challenges. As she began to distinguish what was within her control and what lived beyond it, she realized what was hers to manage was her response to life's challenges. In the face of anger, she learned to pause, consider, and then decide what she wanted to do. Gradually, Selissa learned how to let go of expectations and accept situations and people as they are. She also learned how to be more present, which contributed to a greater sense of gratitude and peace.

The choice to seek out therapy to help address emotional pain, mental anguish, behavioral patterns that need to be unpacked, and the impact of trauma—whether physical, emotional, complex, or generational—is truly transformative. You may think you don't "qualify" for therapy, but if you resonate with any of these you may wish to think again:

- Trouble getting started on or finishing a project
- Fear of commitment
- Perfectionism
- People-pleasing
- Difficulty making decisions
- An overdeveloped sense of responsibility
- Social anxiety
- Inability to say no
- Distrust
- Feeling disconnected from your emotions or your body
- Outsized emotional responses
- Regular sense of "fight," "flight," or "freeze"
- Difficulty with authority
- Lying
- Exaggerating or minimizing the importance of things
- Low self-worth or feeling that you "don't belong"
- Ever-present or major outbursts of anger
- Heightened sense of threat perception

My first interaction with a therapist came roughly twenty years ago and in a moment of big crisis: I had just experienced a panic attack—my first—and didn't understand what was happening to my body or my mind. A coworker ran down from our nineteenth-story office to rescue me from the spot where I was stuck shivering on a street corner between my office and a client's office, and pulled me into the nearest warm building, a bank, where we sat in chairs in the middle of the lobby. That dear friend, whose kindness that day I won't ever forget, watched me sob and talked me down until I could breathe again. After I returned to myself, weary and shaken and so confused, she pressed into my hand the phone number to a therapist that I would call later that day, and continue to use on and off for the next several years.

That therapist, Valorie, was the gift I didn't even know I needed.

She validated my experience, normalized and contextualized it, gave me language for what I didn't know how to express. Working with her was the first time I realized I wasn't alone in my thoughts and feelings and reactions and patterns, that I couldn't be alone if I tried. She challenged me to try things differently, gave me new ways of seeing and new legs for standing on. She helped to unwind so much that had, over many years, become tightly wound up within me.

Valorie was one of my first calls when I learned my father was dying and when he passed two years later; as I considered whether to leave my job; in the early stages of my sobriety; and when my marriage fell apart. At that point, she transitioned from being my individual therapist to seeing Dave and me as a couple.

Over nearly a year and a half, she helped us both make sense of what had brought us to the point of seeking counseling, seeing ourselves and our past with a gentleness and understanding neither of us had possessed before, and guiding us through evaluating the marriage we had against the kind of marriage we wanted. In the end, it was a mutual choice to part, and the grace we were able to show one another through that process remains one of the most beautiful experiences of my life. I thank her still for facilitating that ending, which led to new beginnings for us both.

During that time, she introduced me to two other women who would play a vital role in my healing: first, a psychiatrist who helped—and still helps—my depression and anxiety through medication; second, a somatic experiencing practitioner, a body-based therapist focused on rebalancing the nervous system.

That deep somatic work, as initially uncomfortable as it was, taught me *literally* how to listen to the upset in my gut, the aches in my head, chills on my skin, tension in my jaw. It enabled me to get in touch with the wisdom of my body in an entirely new way, opening floodgates and releasing decades of held trauma and grief that I had worked so diligently to stuff down.

After Dave and I divorced and I remarried a few years later, I turned to a different kind of counselor, one who specialized in family relationships and could help me, my husband Martin, and our four children begin the blending of what we affectionately call "The Wolf Den." We learned from Carolyn so much about parenting styles and techniques that we continue to apply today. Further, she helped me see more of my own trauma responses and ongoing dysregulation in my nervous system. For as much as I felt like I was living in the present, it became clear there was much deeper work to do to understand and heal from my past.

More scared than I cared to admit, I didn't immediately take the dive Carolyn recommended, trying instead to keep treading water closer to the surface. It didn't work—*of course it didn't work!*—and all the whirling and swirling of a chaotic period caught up with me. (I mean, leaving a career, quitting alcohol, ending a marriage, falling in love and remarrying, moving into a new home, and blending a family with four kids in elementary school—all within five short years—ain't for sissies.) Eventually I found myself locked in a depression that, no matter what tools I threw at it, refused to budge. For several months.

My first therapist had moved by then, so I did what many people do when they're starting from scratch and searched the *Psychology Today* database for a profile that would match with what I needed: licensed in my state; on my insurance plan; with experience in anxiety, depression, trauma, and inner-child work.

I found a few who didn't check all the boxes but might "do" and then, to my surprise, came across one who checked every box and then some. And what a match! My growth with Tracie has been deep and wide. Even after all these years, every session offers a new aha, a new healing. (*Please, woman, please—never retire.*)

What's been the biggest difference maker about this stint is that it has been more of a constant than a blip, not the reactive oh-lordy-I'm-in-the-shitstorm-again mode, and I go whether I want to or not.

And the thing is, I *do* want to.

When we are no longer afraid of what there is to uncover, when truth grows more precious than appearances, when we understand that nothing can destroy our divinity—that's when it becomes a joy to meet all the parts of ourselves. *It is what it is* and *now it's like this*. Acceptance and contentment, even when there is hard work to do.

I share all of this—even my therapists' first names—not because I have some weird predilection for the airing of so-called dirty laundry, but because we have got to normalize seeking help when we need it.

The pandemic certainly pushed more people toward therapy, but that's only because it pushed them to the brink first: A November 2021 survey by *The New York Times* revealed 90 percent of therapists surveyed in the U.S. reported an increase in the number of people seeking therapy since COVID-19, with 75 percent reporting long wait times to see new patients. A third reported it could take at least three months before they could offer an appointment, if they had room for new patients at all. "Every available time slot I can offer is filled," one therapist said.[16]

It's time to encourage therapy as more than crisis management. As a society, the more we can reduce the sense of stigma and shame, particularly for men and older generations and people of color, the more healing can occur. The less secret and more accessible and affordable, especially in underserved and economically disadvantaged communities, the more widespread the benefit.

So here is my ask of you: If you think it would resonate with another, share your story of healing through therapy. Share *my* story if it might help someone make that call. And, if *you* are struggling as you read this, please don't go through the struggle alone. Help awaits.

Journaling

The other practice I recommend turning to when thoughts and feelings demand to be heard, unpacked, and nurtured is a hot date with your journal. Like therapy, writing is most helpful when habitual and not just a fury we unleash in crisis mode (although there is great power in that release, too).

Writing is an instrument of healing, and healing can occur faster when we tend to it regularly rather than in fits and starts.

> Writing is an instrument of healing, and healing can occur faster when we tend to it regularly rather than in fits and starts.

By "writing" I don't mean books or scholarly articles or anthology-ready poems, but rather journal entries, lists— anything that takes the words and feelings out of your head and makes some kind of sense of them on the page.

Why is the act of writing so therapeutic? Simple: it get the two sides of our brains working in concert.

"To tell a story that makes sense, the left brain must put things in order, using words and logic. The right brain

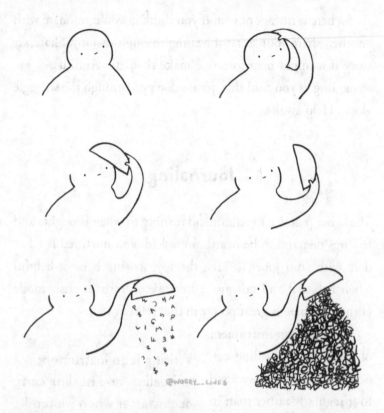

contributes the bodily sensations, raw emotions, and personal memories, so we can see the whole picture and communicate our experience," wrote Daniel Siegel in *The Whole-Brain Child*. "This is the scientific explanation behind why journaling and talking about a difficult event can be so powerful in helping us heal. In fact, research shows that merely assigning a name or label to what we feel literally calms down the activity of the emotional circuitry of the right hemisphere."[17]

The act of attaching language to emotions—which is what we do when we translate that nebulous, knotted, writhing jumble of perceptions gyrating in the mind into words of substance and nuance—allows us to begin to process so much that was previously either unexamined, misinterpreted, or unexpressed.

While we might hope to sit down at the blank page and channel some gorgeous, flowing, poetic word garland, more often than not what is released to the paper reflects that jumble that we're still making sense of. ("I write entirely to find out what I'm thinking, what I'm looking at, what I see and what it means. What I want and what I fear,"[18] Joan Didion wrote.)

The value of journaling is the process, not the finished product. It does not have to be elegant or lucid and is for your eyes only.

Julia Cameron, of "morning pages" fame, wrote in *The Artist's Way* that the point of a private, unedited release to the page is to "sort through the differences between our real feelings, which are often secret, and our official feelings, those on the record for public display."[19] An undignified metaphor, perhaps, but I think of it as a mental dump truck backing up—*beep, beep, beep!*—to release the load of crap we carry around. And, once empty, something fresh can arise in its place.

In her most excellent book *How the Light Gets In: Writing as a Spiritual Practice*, Pat Schneider, a Missouri girl like me, wrote: "To write about what is painful is to begin the work of healing."[20] There are, however, days when the best anyone can come up with is a profane yell. (Personally, I have begun many a session with my favorite word, which may or may not start with an F, repeated in various forms, unparalleled in its ability to convey my deepest thoughts. You are welcome to borrow this technique anytime. Talk about therapeutic!)

What I try to give to the page as I work through a question, or set down a heavy hurt, or dream about what the future might hold for my children and their children, is the truth as I know it. Objectivity is beyond reason in the context of discharge; it all flows through the filter of my understanding before landing on the ground. But then, once my eyes can process in black and white what my heart could only see in searing technicolor, there is something to work with. First the release, then the effort to make any sense from it. Kind of like therapy, eh?

Comfort and Rest

In 2016, BBC Radio 4 and researchers at Durham University in the UK collaborated to conduct the world's largest-ever survey on the topic of rest, with 18,000 respondents from 134 countries. It was dubbed, appropriately, "The Rest Test."[21] Not surprisingly, more than two-thirds of those surveyed said they did not get enough rest in their lives.

What was rather unexpected, though, is that when respondents were asked to identify the activities they found *most* restful, what they ranked highest is typically done alone.

"When we say we need more rest," the study's authors concluded, "is it that we yearn for time away from other people." C. S. Lewis posited largely the same thing eighty years ago: "We live, in fact, in a world starved for solitude, silence, and private: and therefore starved for meditation and true friendship."[22]

Here are the activities respondents identified as most restful:

1. Reading
2. Being in (or looking at images of) the natural environment
3. Being on your own
4. Listening to music
5. Doing nothing in particular
6. Walking
7. Having a bath or shower
8. Daydreaming
9. Watching TV
10. Meditating or practicing mindfulness

Years ago, you could coax me into bed during the middle of the day only if I was sick enough to stay home from work; nowadays, you might just find me there enjoying a little catnap on a random Wednesday afternoon, just because. I'm known to take a shower for reasons completely unrelated to hygiene, put my feet up with a warm and weighted flaxseed pillow on my lap, settle down on the floor and let the cats crawl all over me, or light a candle and just gaze out the window for ten minutes.

Comfort, rest, and time alone sustain us no less than the food we eat and water we drink. That's why I have learned to feel a sense of *accomplishment*, not *guilt*, when I take steps to recharge.

In the same way that many of us aren't fluent in the language of emotions because no one ever taught it to us, far too many of us lack the ability to take comfort and rest because it's not regularly modeled or practiced in our Western culture. We confuse self-discipline with self-denial, pervert a strong work ethic into an unsustainable attitude of "all work and no play," and glorify busy-ness instead.

But rest is not laziness!

In yoga, the most important pose comes at the end of a practice. Called "corpse pose" (*savasana*), this is the closing period of lying flat on the floor, when we allow body and mind to integrate at a time when both are still. Not sleeping but *resting*. This time is built into the experience on the mat, not left for anyone to try and work in on their own time. *Rest is simply part of the practice.*

And now, my friend, you must learn to rest, too.

Rest can mean different things. Sometimes it's a hard stop for the body, like slipping into bed when you're physically worn down. Other times, it's a respite from the nonstop buzzing of life—breathing space, if you will. All the time, it is the opposite of "being on," whether socially, emotionally, or mentally.

Rest is to our being what rain is to the garden. No rain means no geranium, no rose, no creeping Jenny spreading and spilling. No rest means no growth, no healing, no inner peace. When we rest, we fortify. But when we deny our Selves the chance to reboot, revive, recalibrate, rejuvenate, regenerate, recover, and reawaken all inside you that is weary, we remain in a state of depletion.

For years I have followed the work of a yoga teacher in Atlanta named Octavia Raheem, an advocate for pausing and resting, particularly for women of color. "Rest is as necessary as breath," Raheem writes in her first book, *Gather*. "Rest allows my heart to remember a slower rhythm. It retrains my cells, nervous system, blood, and muscles to trust that there can be rest for the weary. I practice restorative yoga for all of the woman within my lineage and within me who need to rest.

"Rest fuels intuition. Rest fuels better choices. Rest fuels breath. Rest fuels clarity. Rest fuels patience. Rest fuels creativity. Rest fuels intimacy. Rest is an honest fuel for our real journey."[23] *An honest fuel for our real journey.*

I hope you walk away from this chapter carrying a deep conviction that Self-care is neither frivolous nor indulgent. It is not narcissistic or greedy. It is, however, smart and sound. If, for whatever reason, you do not nurture your Self, you risk becoming worn and wearied, hollow in the shell, unable to maintain any energy in the moment, much less move forward with vigor.

> Self-care is neither frivolous nor indulgent. It is not narcissistic or greedy. It is, however, smart and sound.

Self-nourishment equals Self-love.

This liminal space you're in represents a spiritual growth spurt. And nourishment during a growth spurt is essential.

There are two ways you can approach Self-love during this liminal time, your growth spurt: you can have it, or not.

Here's what it looks like to *not* love your Self: Head out on a cross-country trip in a beater of a car, on four flat tires with no spare, in the heat with no air conditioning, in the rain with no windshield wipers, in the snow with no chains; the gas tank *this close* to empty and a thousand miles to go before the next service station; no snacks, no water, no bathroom, and nothing but static on the radio. Sure, you *can* make it that way, but there is an alternative that makes more sense.

To love your Self, on the other hand, means to give your Self every resource that will help you be as successful as possible: full tires, full tank, full belly, full heart.

Why would you choose to do it any other way?

Closing Exercise: Caring for Your Sweet Self in Times of Change

In this liminal time, how will you fill the "doctor's orders" of regularly purifying and fortifying your body, mind, and spirit for more energy, clarity, and peace? How can you better incorporate the practices explored in this chapter—movement and breath, mindfulness and meditation, letting go, cultivating emotional intelligence, regular therapy, journaling, and rest—for your benefit? What specific Self-care actions will you add to your playbook? And, like the other steps outlined here, how will you stay accountable to your Self?

10

Putting It All Together

A ship in harbor is safe. But that's not what ships are built for.
—John Augustus Shedd

W ell, gang. That's all I've got. Time to toss this puppy in the ol' recycle bin.

Wait! Don't you dare!

When I need a little hit of perspective or solace or inspiration or confirmation, I routinely lean over to the bookcase to the right of my desk, pluck a certain title off the shelf—I always know *just* the one I'm looking for—and thumb straight to a highlighted passage on a well-read page. Cracks in the spines tell me where to go, and my heart gets exactly what she needs in that moment.

Among the four hundred or so titles in my possession, there are perhaps a dozen that serve as Bibles for my growth. (You'll find a list of those resources at the end.)

I want this to be such a book for *you*.

If you need to be reminded that you're not alone in feeling stuck, go right back to Chapter 1.

If your Pipsqueak Twerp needs a muzzle, flip to Chapter 4. Confused about who you *really* are? Head to Chapter 5.

You can return here as many times as you like. There is no limit, no expiration date. This book is here for as long as you need it.

When I launched You Are Not Stuck in 2014, I thought of the name as a mindset, a mantra, an ethos. A permission. A rally cry. Something I might just tattoo on my body to remind me of the choices that are always before me. (You never know, I still might. These arms aren't full yet.)

But as I had the opportunity to put the principles into practice in my own life—not once, but several times—it became clear that I had also birthed something of a process. By that I don't mean "5 Easy Steps to Freedom! Get Happy or Your Money Back!" What I organized is a strategic framework to reevaluate life when it feels uninspired or arduous or wholly intolerable—and, when things are indeed out of alignment, to help folks tap into the wisdom and courage they already possess in order to make important choices. (To paraphrase Glinda the Good Witch to Dorothy: "You've always had the power, my dear, you just had to learn it for yourself.")

What is most valuable about this framework is that it doesn't just work in a crisis. It works just as well when you contemplate the questions as regular reflection: *What's working? What's not? How do I feel and what do I need? What's got to change?* You can repeat the process often, applying it to major obstacles and more humble ones, too.

This kind of ongoing evaluation—faithfully tending to life, pulling the proverbial weeds, keeping the right balance of sun and shade, watering regularly, fertilizing often, repotting when necessary—is what I call "constant gardening." The garden stays lush when we care for it. When we don't, it suffers.

The same applies to our being. When we ignore our needs and the signs of our suffering, we, too, will wilt and wither and decay. When it's almost too late, there's often a desperate last-gasp effort—something you might call a midlife crisis.

But you don't have to wait for a crisis or catastrophe or any kind of rock-bottom breaking point to begin living your life with intention. *You just have to begin living your life with intention.* As Wordsworth said, "To begin, begin."

> You don't have to wait for a crisis or catastrophe or any kind of rock-bottom breaking point to begin living your life with intention. *You just have to begin living your life with intention.*

It takes a great personal audacity to question the status quo, to take exception to it, to redefine it, and, ultimately, decide for your Self what "normal" is going to be. But guess what? That autonomy to choose your own circumstances is your birthright.

Procrastination, that insolent little wench, may tell you, "Not yet." Fear may say it's impossible. Your Pipsqueak Twerp will likely add some shitty lie like, "You don't deserve it anyway, so why even bother?"

But as some wise soul said, "Procrastination is like masturbation: it's fun for a while, but in the end, you're only screwing yourself."

So don't listen to them. Listen to me. Listen to your Self.

Here's an at-a-glance recap of the nine steps outlined in this book, organized by chapter, which you can revisit anytime you'd like.

1. The Empowerment Gap: Start by understanding where you're feeling stuck and how that impacts your day-to-day life.

2. Indigestion of Shoulds: Articulate clearly, perhaps for the first time, what it is you don't want in this life.

3. Know What You Want Instead: Understand the life you do desire, and why.

4. How Fear Holds You Back: Name and face squarely the fears that keep you stagnant.

5. Who Do You Think You Are: Recognize and leverage your divine inner badass.

6. The Power of Soul-Guided Choices: Know the difference between deciding from your fear and choosing from your soul.

7. Trade-offs, Consequences, and Boundaries: They're inevitable; might as well anticipate so you can encounter them with eyes wide open.

8. The Playbook: This strategic, detailed, personalized playbook will guide your next moves.

9. Care for the Journey: The liminal space you're in
   requires nurturance, grounding, and healing; make
   sure you love your Self enough to provide it.

If you're less of a "process" kind of person and more of a
bumper-sticker-wisdom type, I've got you covered.

I love bumper stickers, though I've only ever put one on a car.
(It read SANTOS MCGARRY, for all you fans of *The West Wing*.)
I love 'em because they're short and memorable, easily digestible
and repeatable. The same applies to slogans on T-shirts and the
quotes I routinely jot down on Post-it Notes and stick to my computer. Insights don't need to be wordy to be wise.

Here are a dozen sayings I'd like you to take away from
this book. Write them down, make bookmarks out of them,
stick them to your mirror or fridge or car visor, wherever they'll
jump out and give you a little pinch of remembering.

- We feel stuck when the life we're living doesn't line up
  with the life we want.
- You deserve the life you dream of rather than one you
  feel stuck in.
- It is never too late to realize the path you've *been* walking
  isn't the one you want to *keep* walking.
- Change starts with acknowledging the life you're living
  isn't the one you want. From there, it's about getting off
  autopilot.
- You're a meat-coated skeleton made of stardust. What do
  you have to be scared of?

- You are badass, bold, and backed by the power of the Universe.
- The opposite of fear isn't just courage. The opposite of fear is choice.
- How bold one is when one is sure of being loved.
- Intention without action is just wishful thinking.
- Just because you get served a shit sandwich doesn't mean you have to eat it.
- Honoring your soul doesn't make you full of yourself; it makes you full of your Self.

Lastly, my favorite, the one that says it all: We all *have* choices; we just have to be brave enough to *make* them.

If you have reached this point in the book and find yourself still asking, "But what if I don't know what my 'not this' is? What if I don't know what needs to change? What if I don't feel ready?"

All I can tell you is this: Keep listening. Your soul will let you know.

The answers are different for each of us, of course. Some of us are like tumbleweeds and made to move on; some of us have a higher tolerance for bullshit and it takes us longer to let go of a bad situation. But, eventually, we all just know.

You'll know when you no longer like your life—or, worse, no longer like yourself.

You'll know when you realize that the fear of an uncertain future is far less daunting than the dreadful pain of sitting still.

You'll know when you can no longer accept crying yourself into madness, or eating yourself into bigger clothes, drinking yourself into oblivion, feeling unspeakably lonely when you're not alone, or hiding in plain sight.

You'll know when your body tells you in unmistakable terms: the gnawing pain in the gut; circles that darken under sleepless eyes or eyes that cry buckets and rivers; the petulant feet that refuse to step one in front of the other or the brave ones that carry us fleeing to a safer place but then can't stop running.

And while there may be a great sense of relief that accompanies the realization that something's got to give, the stress that your body and psyche have been under all this time doesn't evaporate overnight. That's where self-care as Self-love comes in.

We talk in yoga about striving to find within a pose the sweet balance between ease and effort (*sukha* and *sthira,* respectively, in Sanskrit). When you are in the process of creating bold change—when you're high above the ground and you've let go of one trapeze bar but haven't yet caught the other—an awful lot of effort is involved.

Pinpointing your "not this" *is effort.*
Defining—and redefining—your values and priorities *is effort.*
Codifying how you want your life to feel rather than look *is effort.*
Getting eye-level with your fears *is effort.*

Accepting that you've got to let some people down in order to honor your Self *is effort*.

Understanding that you are freakin' God (!) *is effort*.

Being ruthlessly honest with yourself *is effort*.

Making an action plan—not to mention the major work that goes into carrying it out—*is effort*.

Please, build in the time and space required to truly nurture your Self. Let this be the ease that balances your effort. Otherwise, you will be lopsided and find yourself walking in circles. Possibly for years.

Trust me on this.

The act of getting unstuck typically doesn't look like a drastic, triumphant, Hollywood moment. It's usually anything but. More often, it's a slow build, the way a single snowflake becomes an avalanche. Your job is to get the first flake in motion. Be patient. Big changes can happen beneath the surface, sometimes when you're not even looking.

Two notes of friendly advice, from someone who's been there:

First, once you muster up the courage to do that thing you've been longing to do, you'll feel proud of yourself, as you should. You'll celebrate for a day or a week or longer, as you should.

But you also might feel a pang of guilt that you didn't make your move earlier, a stab of regret that you wasted precious, unrecoverable time. Please don't do that. Guilt and regret will do nothing to propel you forward, they'll only keep you connected to what you were trying to shake off in the past.

Second, don't get too satisfied too quickly and allow complacency to take root, which is a natural response after making some progress. *Natural,* but not *helpful;* think of the way you might not finish a ten-day prescription of antibiotics after you start feeling better. We often confuse improvement with cure, "not that bad" with "pretty damn good." But if you're not yet feeling the way you want to, the way you identified back in Chapter 3, keep going. Remember your *why.* Remember the freedom you seek.

That's what this journey is all about—becoming free.

Free to decide, free to shape, free to explore.

Free to break out of a world governed by Other People's perceptions, values, expectations, priorities, norms, measurements.

Free to shed all the rules you observe but didn't write.

Free to make mistakes and free to try again.

Free to prioritize and reorganize yourself.

Free to say no so you can say yes.

Free to be happy.

Free to be your Self.

Free to choose a life so rich and luscious that, as the poet Nayyirah Waheed wrote, it is "dripping down your chin."[1]

As you go about this important work, remember:

You are not stuck. Nor are you broken. You are not weak. You are not lost.

You are not powerless or speechless or stranded, or deadlocked with the parts of yourself you wish to change.

You are not too different or too complicated or too sad. You are not beyond repair, or the sum total of your past mistakes. You are not the coulds or the shoulds or the woulds.

Have mercy on yourself.

What you are is human . . . and humans are fragile and strong and beautiful and wild.

You're also divine. It is within this undivided dichotomy of human and God that we seek and find, feel and heal, expand and contract in a spiral.

Some days will be harder than others. They may even threaten to break you. But they won't. They can't. For you are indestructible, and every part of you is a miracle.

Most of all, darling, know this:

You are not the stars you reached for but didn't catch. *You are the reaching.*

And you get to reach for as many stars as you like, until your last breath.

Epilogue

While this book isn't a memoir *per se,* there is enough personal revelation and reflection that you might have flipped that last page curious about how my story ends, like when the final scene of a true-life movie fades to black and you think: "I wonder what happened to *that* guy!?"

Well, first of all, this little story of mine is far from over. New chapters are being written every day, thank God, because the returns of seeking and the joy of healing keep coming—one character, one word, one breath at a time. But if you're looking for evidence that the process I've laid out for you actually *works,* then, yeah, I've got some proof points.

Like no more "Sunday night scaries," those moments of dread that rise up from your belly and close around your throat from the inside when you know the Monday morning ahead of you is not the Monday morning you want.

Like gratitude that the work of a random Tuesday is helping people find the magic that lives in their lungs and their spirit, rather than helping a big corporation spin their version of the truth.

Like a head on the pillow at night that's no longer swimming in self-hatred or regurgitating regret, but instead content with the knowledge that I lived up to my Self on this day gone, and looking forward to doing it again the next.

A marriage in which there's no doubt whether I'm loved, and I don't think I'll ever be kissed for the last time.

A breath, a body, a mindset rooted in steadiness and ease.

Is there still work to do? *Oh, hell yes!* But it doesn't feel like work anymore. It feels like purpose. Like alchemy. Like *love* to sprinkle all over the goddamn place.

And I love you. Thank you for reading.

Acknowledgments

The process of nurturing a book from seed to fruit is unlike anything I've ever known.

The idea for this project first appeared back in 2014. I started on a proposal and, the following year, pitched a handful of literary agents. When one expressed interest, I did what many tenderhearted, doubt-filled, depressed humans might do: a brief happy dance, with a clap on my own back . . . and then I walked straight over to my bed, crawled in, and drew the covers over my head. *Literally.* Then, even when I emerged, this book remained in that metaphorical space for years, and I was saturated with the frustration that I didn't have it in me to move this forward.

But in 2021, when the Universe knew the time was right, she opened up the path in the way the Bible describes Moses's parting of the Red Sea. All the pieces magically fell into place. And this reminded me that fruit ripens on its own time, that a dream delayed is not a dream discarded. Experiences must incubate before we can make real sense of them. Detours do not necessarily translate to being lost.

I finished this book mostly in isolated pandemic times, but still with a great deal of encouragement and support over many years prior. To every friend who ever cheered me on, inquired with genuine interest, "How's the book coming along?," left a reassuring comment on social media, talked through a concept, or provided feedback on an idea or a passage: thank you, most sincerely.

I offer special thanks to my incredible literary agent, Alexander Field, and his team at The Bindery. You took a chance on me and my work and suffered my inexhaustible first-time-author questions with great patience. (Anyone who knows me will attest that my questions are, indeed, inexhaustible.) The same thanks goes to my outstanding editor, Hannah Phillips, at St. Martin's Press. You believed in this project from the beginning and guided it to completion so deftly. You are a stellar being, my dear. May we make many books together.

In the year before this book was completed, a medium told me part of the reason it was slowgoing was because my circle of support wasn't quite full and that I needed to bring in three women. Betsy Rapoport, Kelly Madrone, and Elissa Altman—clearly she meant you. Thank you, each of you, for your savvy insights, honest feedback, brilliant pens, and encouragement along the way.

Amy Calvin, your mentorship and friendship have been a constant in my life for nearly two decades, and I count on you more than you even know. There is no one else I would rather walk with in The Wilderness. God wants what you have.

To all the yoga teachers who have taught and inspired me, especially Pam Schulte and Kitty Daly, Tias Little, and Elena Brower, and the magnificent generation of writers that is Elizabeth Gilbert, Brené Brown, Cheryl Strayed, Glennon Doyle, and

Rob Bell: I carry your wisdom in my heart and it is a tremendous honor to pass it on to others. Jennifer Pastiloff, thank you for being a real, beautiful example of what is possible.

I want to thank all my FHriends, colleagues, mentors—particularly the one and only Rich Eichwald, who taught me the valuable lesson of "start in the middle and leave lots of holes" and the truth of "shit works out." Also, to Chelsey Ilten and Marisa Giller: you've no idea how much I enjoy being the cool aunt. I love you both, forever.

Scott Stabile, my soul brother, you and your love are bright lights in this world. That you have turned your pain into wisdom and grace for others is a gift we are all thankful for. Thank you for carrying me through the difficult times and for making the good times even sweeter.

Mike Spakowski, you and the team at Atomicdust have so generously given me encouragement, ideas, and a presence on the World Wide Web. Someday I will pay you in more than frozen key lime pies; until then, please know how much your help has mattered.

Jim Zartman, you heard the authority in my voice before I did and reminded me what was important: THIS. Your insights and unique way of helping people stand taller are remarkable, and the sticky note with your words "calm effort" remains posted to my computer monitor.

Deep gratitude to the talent that is Worry Lines and the illustration you created for this book. You inspire and delight.

To each and every individual who has trusted me over the years with your pain, your secrets, your fears, your deepest desires—whether in a yoga practice, a workshop, retreat, online class, walk and talk, phone call, or private message—I want to extend my deepest and most humble gratitude. It is a privilege to hold that precious space for you, and one I don't take lightly. I send extra appreciation to those who so graciously allowed me to include their stories in this book.

I owe so much to my sober community, wide and varied as it is: the women of Thank God It's Monday; LL; my favorite HOMEies Tammi Salas, Natalie Austin, and Hilary Massicotte; all the members of The Luckiest Club, especially Lisa Williams, Mike Breen, Tammi Scott; my cherished Blue Diamond Girls; and every single one of my sisters and brothers in sobriety, in pain, in grief, in shame, in depression, in divorce, in anxiety, in paralysis, in searching, in finding, in healing. This is for us. What once felt like something that set us apart is actually the truth that stitches us together. Forever bound. Forever in solidarity.

Valorie Adrio and Tracie Wallace, for all the ways you have taught me to understand myself, integrate myself, love myself . . . you have my sincere and unending appreciation.

Back in 1985, my sixth-grade teacher at St. Bernadette's Catholic Grade School in St. Louis, Sister Theresa, made a habit (ha!) of trying to correct my frequent misbehavior with writing assignments. In the process, she sparked within me a love of pen across page and the belief that maybe, someday, somehow, I might make a thing of it. The school is long closed and I suspect she is long gone, too, but still: thank you. Same to my journalism professors and mentors, Don Corrigan and the late Ed Bishop of Webster University.

To my parents, all three of them; I hold sincere gratitude for the lessons learned through our relationships. Also, Katie, Johnny, and Annie, whose stories are intertwined with mine. Sis, I offer you a deepest bow for all the years you cared for your brother, my father. Speaking of family, this may be unorthodox, but I want to thank all the animals with whom I've had the privilege of sharing my life and home. The comfort, companionship, and delight you have given me over the years is immeasurable.

Finally, my Wolf Pack: Martin, my best friend, my sea, my king, my idiot. My husband. Your steadiness (like God's) is the antidote to my hummingbird nature. We are testament to the power of soul-guided choices and I hold your heart fiercely and tenderly. I will and I do, every day. Braeden and Greyson, you are the sons I didn't know I needed. I love you so.

And, lastly, my beautiful daughters, Josie and Julia, the fruit born from my body. Without you, this gorgeous life I know now would not have been possible. You are the ones who changed me, who broke me open, who set me straight, and it is the privilege of privileges that you call me Mother. You are my everything. I adore you, Chickens, forever and ever.

Recommended Resources

The Gifts of Imperfection by Brené Brown

The Untethered Soul by Michael Singer

How Will You Measure Your Life? by Clayton Christensen

Codependent No More by Melody Beattie

How the Light Gets In by Pat Schneider

The Body Keeps the Score by Bessel van der Kolk

Emotional Sobriety by Tian Dayton

Tiny Beautiful Things by Cheryl Strayed

Set Boundaries, Find Peace by Nedra Glover Tawwab

How to Do the Work by Nicole LePera

The RobCast podcast by Rob Bell

Works Cited (Epigraphs)

Brower, Elena. Yoga workshop in St. Louis, Missouri. February 2015.

Carnegie, Dale. *How to Win Friends and Influence People*. New York: Simon & Schuster, 1936.

Chödrön, Pema. *Comfortable With Uncertainty: 108 Teachings on Cultivating Fearlessness and Compassion*. Boulder, CO: Shambhala, 2018.

Jenkins, Jedidiah. *Like Streams to the Ocean: Notes on Ego, Love, and the Things That Make Us Who We Are*. New York: Convergent Books, 2021.

Lamott, Anne. *Help, Thanks, Wow: The Three Essential Prayers*. New York: Riverhead Books, 2012.

Raheem, Octavia. *Pause, Rest, Be: Stillness Practices for Courage in Times of Change*. New York: Penguin Random House, 2022.

Schneider, Pat. *How the Light Gets In: Writing as a Spiritual Practice*. Oxford, UK: Oxford University Press, 2013.

Shedd, John Augustus. *Salt from My Attic*. Mosher Press, 1928.

Singer, Michael A. *The Untethered Soul: The Journey Beyond Yourself*. Oakland, CA: New Harbinger Publications and Noetic Books, 2007.

Stabile, Scott. *Just Love*. McCarren Park Publishing, 2015.

Strayed, Cheryl. *Tiny Beautiful Things: Advice on Love and Life from Dear Sugar*. New York: Vintage Books, 2012.

Notes

Introduction

1. Carson, Rachel. *Silent Spring.* New York: Fawcett World Library, 1962, 12.

2. Torontow, Alexa. "When We Get Quiet Enough." Reproduced by permission from the author.

Chapter 1: The Empowerment Gap

1. Vollmer, Becky. "You Are Not Stuck" survey, via Survey Monkey. February 2015.

2. "'Leap Day' Survey Identifies America's Wish List Of Most Popular Aspirations," GoDaddy Inc., February 29, 2016, https://www.prnewswire.com/news-releases/leap-day-survey-identifies-americas-wish-list-of-most-popular-aspirations-300228101.html.

3. Sifferlin, Alexandra. "Here's How Happy Americans Are Right Now," *Time,* July 26, 2017, https://time.com/4871720/how-happy-are-americans/.

4. "Just three in 10 people feel 'happy with their lives,'" *The Telegraph,* January 22, 2015, https://www.telegraph.co.uk/news/uknews/11362246/Just-three-in-10-people-feel-happy-with-their-lives.html.

5. "Antidepressant Use Among Persons Aged 12 and Over: United States, 2011–2014," National Center for Health Statistics Data Brief No. 283, August 2017, https://www.cdc.gov/nchs/products/databriefs/db283.htm.

6. Clopton, Jennifer. "Alcohol Consumption Among Women Is on the Rise," *WebMD,* July 18, 2018, https://www.webmd.com/women/news/20180718 /alcohol-consumption-among-women-is-on-the-rise.

7. Rodrick, Stephen. "All-American Despair," *Rolling Stone,* May 30, 2019, https://www.rollingstone.com/culture/culture-features/suicide-rate-america -white-men-841576/.

8. Wong, May. "Stanford research provides a snapshot of a new working-from-home economy," Stanford University, June 29, 2020, https://news .stanford.edu/2020/06/29/snapshot-new-working-home-economy/.

Chapter 2: Indigestion of Shoulds

1. Dayton, Tian. *Emotional Sobriety: From Relationship Trauma to Resilience and Balance.* Health Communications, Inc., 2007.

2. Gilbert, Elizabeth. "NOT THIS," Facebook, April 12, 2016, https://m .facebook.com/GilbertLiz/posts/not-this-back-by-popular-demandsweet -friends-for-some-mysterious-reason-that-i-s/1004594839622631/.

Chapter 3: Know What You Want Instead

1. The Avett Brothers, "Head Full of Doubt/Road Full of Promise," lyrics © BMG Rights Management, 2009.

2. Plimpton, George. "E. L. Doctorow, The Art of Fiction No. 94," *The Paris Review,* No. 94, Issue 101, Winter 1986, https://www.theparisreview.org /interviews/2718/the-art-of-fiction-no-94-e-l-doctorow.

3. Bell, Rob. "South Star," *The RobCast,* Ep. 303, March 12, 2021, audio, 9:40, https://robbell.podbean.com/e/south-star/.

4. Coulter, Kristi. *Nothing Good Can Come from This.* New York: Farrar, Straus and Giroux, 2018, 10.

5. Clear, James. *Atomic Habits: An Easy & Proven Way to Build Good Habits & Break Bad Ones.* New York: Avery, 2018, 38.

6. Dillard, Annie. *The Writing Life.* New York: Harper & Row, 1989, 32.

7. Christensen, Clayton M. "How Will You Measure Your Life?" *Harvard Business Review,* July–August, 2010.

8. Whyte, David. "Sometimes," copyrighted material used with permission of author.

Chapter 4: How Fear Holds You Back

1. Kross, Ethan. *Chatter: The Voice in Our Head, Why It Matters, and How to Harness It.* New York: Crown, 2021, xxii.

2. Singer, Michael A. *The Untethered Soul: The Journey Beyond Yourself.* Oakland, CA: New Harbinger Publications and Noetic Books, 2007, 82–83.

3. "Why Brené Brown Says Perfection Is a 20-Ton Shield." YouTube, uploaded by Oprah Winfrey Network, 6 October 2013, 3:10, https://www.youtube.com/watch?v=o7yYFHyvweE.

Chapter 5: Who Do You Think You Are?

1. Satchidananda, Sri Swami. *Integral Yoga: The Yoga Sutras of Patanjali.* Buckingham, VA: Integral Yoga Publications, 1978.

2. "How Yoga Helps Heal Trauma: A Q&A with Bessel van der Kolk." Kripalu Center for Yoga & Health, https://kripalu.org/resources/how-yoga-helps-heal-trauma-qa-bessel-van-der-kolk.

3. Pransky, Jillian. *Deep Listening: A Healing Practice to Calm Your Body, Clear Your Mind, and Open Your Heart.* New York: Rodale Books, 2017.

4. Williams, J. Mark G., John Teasdale, Zindel Segal, and Jon Kabat-Zinn. *The Mindful Way Through Depression: Freeing Yourself from Chronic Unhappiness.* New York: Guilford Press, 2007.

Chapter 6: The Power of Soul-Guided Choices

1. Easwaran, Eknath. *Essence of the Upanishads: A Key to Indian Spirituality.* Tomales, CA: Nilgiri Press, 2009.

2. Brown, Brené. *Dare to Lead: Brave Work. Tough Conversations. Whole Hearts.* New York: Random House, 2018.

3. Brown, Jeff. *Ascending with Both Feet on the Ground: Words to Awaken Your Heart.* Ontario, CA: Enrealment Press, 2012.

Chapter 7: Trade-Offs, Consequences, and Boundaries

1. Tawwab, Nedra Glover. *Set Boundaries, Find Peace: A Guide to Reclaiming Yourself.* New York: TarcherPerigee, 2021.

Chapter 8: The Playbook

1. Bushnell, Nolan with Gene Stone. *Finding the Next Steve Jobs: How to Find, Keep, and Nurture Talent.* New York: Simon & Schuster, 2013.

2. Rubin, Gretchen. *The Four Tendencies: The Indispensable Personality Profiles That Reveal How to Make Your Life Better (and Other People's Lives Better, Too).* New York: Harmony, 2017.

3. Clear, *Atomic Habits*, 18.

4. Clear, *Atomic Habits*, 38.

5. Erickson, Victoria (@victoriaericksonwriter). Instagram photo, October 26, 2016, https://www.instagram.com/p/BMC9oxvDTLf/.

6. Alcoholics Anonymous. *Alcoholics Anonymous: The Big Book.* Alcoholics Anonymous World Services, 1939, 58.

7. Francis-Tan, Andrew and Hugo M. Mialon. "'A Diamond is Forever' and Other Fairy Tales: The Relationship between Wedding Expenses and Marriage Duration," September 15, 2014, https://ssrn.com/abstract =2501480.

8. Palmer, Amanda. *The Art of Asking: How I Learned to Stop Worrying and Let People Help.* New York: Grand Central Publishing, 2014, 303.

Chapter 9: Care for the Journey

1. Levin, Nancy. *Jump . . . And Your Life Will Appear: An Inch-by-Inch Guide to Making a Major Change.* New York: Hay House, 2014.

2. Plett, Heather. *The Art of Holding Space: A Practice of Love, Liberation, and Leadership.* Vancouver, BC: Page Two Books, 2020, 24.

3. Plett. *The Art of Holding Space*, 139.

4. Haig, Matt. *The Comfort Book.* New York: Penguin Life, 2021.

5. Nagoski, Emily and Amelia Nagoski. *Burnout: The Secret to Unlocking the Stress Cycle.* New York: Ballantine Books, 2019.

6. Divine, Mark. *The Way of the SEAL: Think Like an Elite Warrior to Lead and Succeed.* Trusted Media Brands, 2013.

7. Iyer, Pico. *The Art of Stillness: Adventures in Going Nowhere.* New York: Simon & Schuster, 2014.

8. Chödrön, Pema. *Comfortable with Uncertainty: 108 Teachings on Cultivating Fearlessness and Compassion.* Boulder, CO: Shambhala, 2002.

9. Chödrön, Pema. *Practicing Peace.* Boulder, CO: Shambhala, 2018.

10. Tolle, Eckhart. *A New Earth: Awakening to Your Life's Purpose.* New York: Penguin Life, 2005.

11. Brach, Tara. *Radical Acceptance: Embracing Your Life With the Heart of a Buddha.* New York: Random House, 2004.

12. Lasater, Judith Hanson. "How to Attract Contentment," *Yoga Journal,* October 11, 2017, https://www.yogajournal.com/yoga-101/philosophy/how -to-attract-contentment-with-judith-hanson-lasater/.

13. Goleman, Daniel. *Emotional Intelligence: Why It Can Matter More Than IQ.* New York: Random House, 2005; McLaren, Karla. *The Language of Emotions: What Your Feelings Are Trying to Tell You.* Louisville, CO: Sounds True, 2010; David, Susan. *Emotional Agility: Get Unstuck, Embrace Change, and Thrive in Work and Life.* New York: Avery, 2016; Brackett, Marc. *Permission to Feel: Unlocking the Power of Emotions to Help Our Kids, Ourselves and Our Society Thrive.* New York: Celadon Books, 2020.

14. McLaren. *The Language of Emotions,* 29.

15. Brackett. *Permission to Feel.*

16. Parker-Pope, Tara, Christina Caron, Mónica Cordero Sancho. "Why 1,320 Therapists Are Worried About Mental Health in America Right Now," *The New York Times,* December 17, 2021, https://www.nytimes.com /interactive/2021/12/16/well/mental-health-crisis-america-covid.html.

17. Siegel, Daniel J., MD, and Tina Payne Bryson, PhD. *The Whole-Brain Child: 12 Revolutionary Strategies to Nurture Your Child's Developing Mind.* New York: Delacorte Press, 2011, 29.

18. Didion, Joan. "Why I Write," *The New York Times,* December 5, 1976, https:// www.nytimes.com/1976/12/05/archives/why-i-write-why-i-write.html.

19. Cameron, Julia. *The Artist's Way: A Spiritual Path to Higher Creativity.* New York: TarcherPerigee, 1992.

20. Schneider, Pat. *How the Light Gets In: Writing as a Spiritual Practice.* Oxford, UK: Oxford University Press, 2013.

21. Hammond, Claudia, and Gemma Lewis. "The Rest Test: Preliminary Findings from a Large-Scale International Survey on Rest," *The Restless Compendium.* 2016. https://doi.org/10.1007/978-3-319-45264-7_8.

22. Lewis, C. S. *The Weight of Glory.* Grand Rapids, MI: Wm. B. Eerdmans Publishing Co., 1965.

23. Raheem, Octavia. *Gather.* Octavia Raheem: 2020, 77–78.

Chapter 10: Putting It All Together

1. Waheed, Nayyirah. *Nejma.* Nayyirah Waheed: 2014.

BECKY VOLLMER is a speaker, yoga teacher, and creator of You Are Not Stuck, a movement that empowers people to pursue the lives they most deeply desire. She guides a global community on social media that is several hundred thousand strong, teaches online courses about empowerment and choice, and leads sold-out programs that combine movement, breathwork, self-exploration, and action planning at yoga and wellness centers across the country. A former newspaper journalist, Becky writes on topics including personal growth, relationships, mental health and wellness, mindfulness, meditation, and spirituality. She also is a leading voice in the sobriety and recovery community. Becky lives in St. Louis, Missouri, with her husband, their four children, three pets, and more flowers than one person should be allowed.